2023

BEACH BUM
"ONE"

Earl Paul

East *of the* Boardwalk

—Collector's Edition—

Earl Paul

Copyright © 2011, 2012, 2014 by Earl Paul

All rights reserved. No part of this book may be used or reproduced in any manner, electronic or mechanical, including photocopying, recording or by any information storage and retrieval system, or otherwise, without written permission from the publisher.

Published by:
ComteQ Publishing
A division of ComteQ Communications, LLC
101 N. Washington Ave. • Suite 1B
Margate, New Jersey 08402
609-487-9000 • Fax 609-487-9099
Email: publisher@ComteQpublishing.com
Website: www.ComteQpublishing.com

ISBN 978-1-935232-21-6
Library of Congress Control Number: 2010930682

Book & cover design: Rob Huberman
Cover photo: Sean M. Fitzgerald
Illustrations: Bobbi Hesiman

Printed in the United States of America

I dedicate this book to my dear and loyal friend, Gary Jessel, who kept me living in this wonderful city for these past years. I am also grateful for the many good friends he allowed me to gather along the way.

To My Dad
Who Dances With Waves

My wake up call
    It's the surf I hear.
The crash of waves
    Get me out of bed.

My feet they bound
    Across the boards.
Soon I will land
    At my home on the sand.

Eyes grow wide
    I watch and study.
Right side left side
    Which way will I ride?

Flippers are on
      My board is in hand
Soon I am gone
      As my feet leave the sand.

Kick kick
      Stroke stroke.
Hurry hurry
      A big one just broke.

I see the swell
      My chance will soon come.
How lucky I feel
      To dance with the waves.

Love,
Tom Paul 2002

(This poem was written by my son and dedicated to me.)

Contents

Preface 9

—1—
A Miracle on the Beach...and *East of the Boardwalk* is Born 11

—2—
"Wait a Minute" 16

—3—
Trouble in Paradise 23

—4—
Her Mom 33

—5—
Why? 37

—6—
Did You Ever... 41

—7—
Wonder... 71

—8—
Lifeguards 72

—9—
When I Am the Mayor... 76

—10—
Beach Wear 78

—11—
Birds of My Beach 85

—12—
Bodyboarding 94

—13—
It's About the Beach 102

—14—
Beach Bum? 106

—15—
Beach Etiquette 110

—16—
Bow Wow City 121

—17—
Bow Wow City: Conclusion 126

—18—
Why Dogs Must Be Banned from Our Beautiful Beaches 129

—19—
Someday Maybe... 131

—20—
Top Ten Reasons Why I Am Always on the Beach 133

—21—
I Give Up 135

—22—
Lucky 136

—23—
Sun of Mine 138

—24—
The One Hundred Yard Forecast 139

—25—
Acceptance and Health 142

—26—
Beautiful Winter 144

—27—
Wicked Winter 145

—28—
Some Suggestions for God 147

—29—
Earl's Favorite Beach Jokes, One-liners, Retorts and Jokes 150

—30—
Lifeguard Humor 155

—31—
The Beach Tag Game 157

—32—
Talk of the Beach 158

—33—
You know it is going to be a bad day at the beach when: 160

—34—
The Game 162

—35—
Number One Beach Bum? 165

—36—
Number One Beach Bum in the World .168

—37—
Recognition 170

—38—
Expanded Recognition 173

—39—
Touching Recognition 175

—40—
Unexpected Recognition 177

—41—
Divine Intervention 179

—42—
The Whale: Why My Beach? 186

—43—
Commandments of the Beach 188

—44—
Looking Back 190

—45—
Big Blue Christmas Eve 193

—46—
"Off Season" – Winter 194

—47—
Late Fall – The Beginning of the Lonely Time 196

—48—
If my umbrella could talk! 198

—49—
Questions I am asked that I don't know the answers to. 200

—50—
Why are you sitting so close to me? 201

—51—
I just don't get it: The Surrey 202

—52—
Dear Sun... 204

—53—
Handicap Access – Where? 206

—54—
I just don't get it: Bicycles 207

—55—
Happiness is... 209

—56—
War on the beach at Plymouth Place 211

—57—
Just have to get some things off my chest 212

—58—
The Second Time Around 215

—59—
The End 217

Around Our Town
with cathy finnegan

Local author Earl Paul shines at OC Library's Author's Tea
Self-professed 'beach bum' shared memories of Ocean City

The Friends & Volunteers of the Ocean City Free Public Library held their annual Author's Dessert Tea at the Flanders on a beautiful spring afternoon. **Karen Bergman** was in the lobby to welcome **Janet Burk, Lori Vitullo, Jean Quaranta** and **Vivian DiMassimo** when they arrived. Good thing the Tea was on a Thursday as these ladies have been playing Mah Jongg on Tuesdays for the past 10 years. **Barbara Weber** was at the top of the stairs to take guests' tickets as they headed down the mirrored hall to the Candlelight Ballroom. **Joan Chapman** stopped to take pictures of the beautiful sandcastle in the center of the hall. **Sandy Crescenzo** chaired the tea again this year, and was tending to last-minute details when guests arrived.

Pat Angarano and **Ginny Coco** are busy getting ready for a charity event benefiting the Cape Shore Chorale, "A Night of Wine & Roses," on Saturday, June 11 and made sure this columnist would be on hand to cover the affair. Pat and Ginny love to sing.

Gwen Pieklo admitted she's no singer, but these members of Holy Trinity Episcopal Church enjoy volunteering at the Clothes Closet. **Sylva Bertini** and husband, **Marino**, are looking forward to celebrating their 54th wedding anniversary June 1 with a tour of London, Ireland, Scotland and France. **Jean Jacobson** is headed for Kennebunkport, Maine to celebrate her birthday the end of May. This is one of her favorite vacation spots and she always stops by and waves to **George and Barbara Bush** at their compound.

Leslie Clarke and **Becky Greene** took a break from folding library events fliers to pose for a picture with this columnist. **Evie Bachich, Elaine Novello** and **Sandy Stango** looked great in bright pink outfits, but I never got them all together for a picture. **Nicollette Mirra**, who has a secret admirer who sent her an orchid, looked stunning in a lime green boucle suit with a matching lime green purse. **Morgan Roberts** thanked me for emailing him his picture with **Meadowlark Lemon**. **Jean Robinson** enjoyed the tea with her Lansdowne High School classmate, **Jean Ruckman**.

Barbara Weber has been going back to college. Last weekend she was at American University when her grandson **Andrew Clark** received his master's degree, and this weekend she'll be at Pitt for granddaughter **Andrea Cote's** graduation.

Andrea Newdeck, Ruth Sukala, Ellen Hagen, Pat Willard, Anne McKenna and their spouses are looking forward to their vacation in Alaska the end of May. **Debbie Sniger** recently moved from the south end to the north end of town.

When Friends & Volun-

Chris Maloney, Evie Bachich, Sandy Crescenzo, Ed Price and Rosemarie Ricci welcome local author Earl Paul.

continued on Page 19

Preface

In fifteen years, Earl believes he has spent more time on the beaches of Ocean City than any other person… ever! In some years, Earl has spent 360 days on the beach. There were some years it was 350. He has weathered all types of conditions to accomplish this incredible feat. Clearing snow in the winter is just another day in paradise.

Earl has seen a lot of things in his fifteen years on the Ocean City beaches. When asked about these interesting things he has recorded, he gets a glimmer his eye and tells of a book he will be writing. "East of the Boardwalk sounds like a good title. "All true, all happened right here on the beach at Plymouth Place."

—1—

A Miracle on the Beach...
and *East of the Boardwalk* is Born

When I don't see my friends for a week or two, they will ask me to tell them a few stories that happened on the beach while they were away. Many times they will say, "Earl, you should write a book." I quickly change the subject because I am probably the last person who you would expect to accomplish such a thing.

When I first started going to the beach, I did see and hear many interesting events. So when I arrived back at my condo, I would write them down in a book. It probably was in my mind that someday I could show them all to my grandchildren.

In late September of 2008, I was sitting with my friend, Frank Maloney, telling him stories about the beach. After I spun a few stories he said, "Earl, you should write a book!" I immediately went into my change-the-subject mode, which caused Frank to jump up and out of his chair.

He looked down at me, and with a raised voice and pointed finger, said, "Let's stop fooling around. You are going to write a book! Now give me a title."

"East of the Boardwalk," I said.

"Oh," he said, "then you were thinking about writing a book after all, weren't you?"

I now knew that I could not run from this challenge. It seemed to be almost impossible, considering the fact that I failed English in high school and writing is not my strong suit.

A couple of days later, I was sitting on the beach, drinking my morning cup of coffee and thinking about writing that darn beach book. How do I start it? What will I say? Will it be fun to read? Will it make sense to other beach people?

I thought and thought but I couldn't even come up with the first sentence. I give up! I should have never agreed to write that book. There will be no book!

And then a miracle happened! I reached down to get my newspaper, which I had tucked under my beach chair. I opened up *The Press of Atlantic City* and there it was in bold black print: "How to write a book!" How could anyone ever explain this coincidence without using the word miracle? Yes, a miracle!

The article was in regards to classes that were being formed at the library in Cape May Court House for older people who wanted to write about their lives. This was so the future generations will know something about them besides old pictures. Eva Feeley, a freelance writer, who just happened to live close by in Sea Isle City, was teaching the class. She was about to start my book.

There was a telephone number in the paper. So I got out my cell phone and proceeded to dial the number. A woman who worked at the library answered the phone and told me that the classes were already full.

"That's okay," I said. "I wasn't going to come anyway, but I would like to talk to Eva Feeley." I gave her my cell phone number and hoped that I would hear from her in a couple days. In less than 30 minutes, my phone rang. It was Eva!

We talked about coming to her next class, but I told her that was not possible. I was going to write a book about a guy who never left the beach, not even to attend classes! I told her my book was going to be about the beach and nothing else.

She thought that it was the first time that anyone had ever done that. I told her I was having trouble getting it started and arranging the telling of my beach stories.

She not only told me how to get started but she raised my confidence level so high that I wanted to run back to my condo and start writing. If she hadn't called me back, I doubt very much if my book would have ever gotten off the ground. She edits all the pages I have completed, then mails them back, with words of encouragement, motivation and wisdom. I was lucky to have people like Frank and Eva. Without them, there would be no *East of the Boardwalk.*

—2—

"Wait A Minute"

How does a guy who was raised in the Frankford section of Philadelphia end up becoming the biggest beach bum in the history of Ocean City?

Did I vacation there when I was a child? No!

Did I have grandparents who took me there in the summer? No!

Was I raised near the Jersey Shore? No!

Did I want to live at the Jersey Shore? Yes!

I often told my wife I wished that I could live at the beach for one year before I died, just to see what it would be like. I am currently on my 15th year and it is even better than I thought.

I lived in a row house in Philadelphia for 60 years. I never saw the sunrise or set. A 12-inch cinder block wall separated my neighbor and me. Living in Ocean City is like being on another planet.

How did I get so lucky? There is no doubt that the stars, planets and the whole universe had to line up. Living at the shore was just a dream, but my dream was about to come true. Soon the sand and ocean would become the center of my universe because of three words:

"Wait a minute."

My wife was the manager of the Palace Roller Skating Center located in the Northeast section of Philadelphia. We were searching for a place at the shore for a weekend. A deliveryman came into my wife's office and she asked him if he knew of any nice condos in Ocean City. He pulled out his wallet and gave her a card with the telephone number of Oceanside Condos. Miracle number one!

The stage was now set. My dream of living at the Jersey Shore was one step closer. It had a heartbeat.

One of the heroes of this story answered the phone. His name was Connor and he worked for Fox Realty. My wife said, "We are looking for a place to stay for the weekend."

"Sorry," Connor said, "but we only rent for the week."

"Oh", my wife said, "we just wanted Friday to Sunday."

Now here is where miracle number two happens.

"Wait a minute," said Connor. "There is a couple that doesn't use their condo. I'll give them a call."

Carl and Lois Cox, owners of condo number 25 said yes.

We were about to start another life on the boardwalk and beaches of Ocean City.

We rented there for about eight weekends, paying a reasonable price of one hundred fifty dollars for two nights. It was a wonderful location – fifty yards from the beach. We were on the third floor, which gave us a great view of Ocean City and the ocean. In the mornings we sat out on the deck drinking our coffee and pinching ourselves to make sure we weren't dreaming.

This is where miracle number three is born. We became good friends with the owners and they would come over often to visit us. We were having a friendly conversation when my unpredictable wife suddenly asked them if they would rent their condo to us year-round.

The Coxes didn't know what to say, they were speechless. "We'll let you know," Carl said. When they left, my nervous wife said, "What did I say? It just came out of my mouth." My wife and I had never once spoken of renting year-round.

"Don't worry, honey, they are not going to do it anyway," I said.

One week later we got the call from Connor. Miracle number three had landed. My dear wife had hit a grand slam home run. The beaches, boardwalk, ocean and condo were now ours, at five hundred dollars a month!

If you follow my story, you will agree that God wanted me to live at the shore. My wife, the deliveryman, Connor and the Coxes were already written in God's big book. Now all I had to do was write the next chapter.

Connor worked for Fox Realty for only one summer, which looks like another part of this miracle. He became a lifeguard on our beaches, which meant that I saw him every day in the summertime for the next 14 years.

Every year I would treat him to a dinner. If he hadn't talked the Coxes into renting their condo, I doubt that I would have ever lived at the Jersey Shore. Connor had changed my life, but he never really understood his role in this story. He just thought that he was doing his job when he called the Coxes.

He has since made the decision to relocate to Florida year-round, which means that my wife, the Coxes and now Connor have gone out of my life. Every day, in some way, I thank them for making my shore life possible.

* * *

Lois and Carl Cox had a house in Pennsylvania and a condo on the bay in Ocean City. We saw them quite often after we rented their condo, but as the years went by we saw them less and less. They sold our condo so my wife and I had to relocate into unit number 30. They also sold their condo on the bay and left Ocean City.

In 2007, I was strolling down the boardwalk on "family night" and someone grabbed my arm. "Remember me?" she asked. It was Lois and Carl. They were vacationing with their kids and grandchildren in Ocean City.

It was hard to believe that it had been 13 years since we first met. They were both in good health and enjoying themselves, which made me quite envious. It brought back a lot of good memories of our arrival in Ocean City. God threw our lives together and changed my life forever.

Sweet Sixteen!

Sunday, April 9, 1950.
Earl and Cass' first Easter together.

—3—
Trouble in Paradise

Now everything was in place for us to begin our "golden years." The condo, beach and boardwalk were all there and our lives were going to be full with enjoyment!

It was June 1995 and we both decided to retire. I had worked for 41 years as a union pipefitter in local union 420. My wife, after raising four kids, became the manager of a large roller skating center in Northeast Philadelphia for 13 years.

We were going to have the perfect life, living four days at our condo in Ocean City and three days at the row house in Philadelphia. How we came to that decision I can't remember, but it didn't take very long to realize that our plan was not going to work. Once we stayed at our condo in Ocean City, it was obvious that we would never return to Philly. We made trips back to our house but never slept in our bed again.

The first day of our retirement, I suggested that we ride bikes like a lot of people do in Ocean City. My wife was a little hesitant, which seemed strange at the time. It got even stranger when she told me to meet her up on the boardwalk with the two 26-inch bikes at the same time. It was very awkward, to say the least.

We got ready to take our first bike ride of the summer and our retirement. I started to pedal down the boardwalk and she was beside me. In less than 30 yards she was spent.

"I can't do it," she said, as she came to a stop. She was panting hard and was out of breath. Thirty yards! I knew right away that this happy life in Ocean City was in deep trouble.

People at the shore ride bikes, walk on the boardwalk and go to the beach. I was about to find out that my wife couldn't do any of these activities.

You may ask how a loving, caring husband allowed his wife's health to deteriorate to a point where she could not pedal a bicycle. That is not an easy question to answer because the problem developed slowly but steadily over a period of 20 to 30 years.

My wife did not like to walk or exercise. Coupled with 40 years of smoking, she was like a time bomb waiting to go off. I still thought that we had many good years ahead of us. My wife being seriously ill was unthinkable.

Like most of us, my wife feared doctors and hospitals. When she had no choice but to seek help, her fears proved to be accurate. She hid her health problems for many years; even our children did not realize how sick she was. This was the life she chose to live until the bicycle episode unmasked the trouble in paradise.

Everyone who met my wife in Ocean City thought that she was a very sociable lady, and she was. However, they didn't know that she couldn't make it to the beach without stopping ten times. On her way to the beach, she would stop and talk to anyone and everyone. She could walk only ten yards at a time without stopping to catch her breath.

Please, young smokers, stop before someone who loves you has to write a story about this problem that had almost made my wife an invalid.

Even though she had this health issue, we still were able to enjoy our retirement. However, her activities were limited and spaced. It was the way she had chosen to live, and I was reluctant to force her to a doctor. In two summers, we had never gone to the boardwalk at night, not even one time! Strange way to live, wasn't it?

I still was able to get to the beach during the summer, and many times my wife got there also. When she did make it to the beach, she thought that I should praise her efforts. She didn't realize that healthy people could walk 40 yards to the beach without any effort. She did not want to admit that she had a problem.

In November of 1997, we went to the casino in Atlantic City like a lot of retirees do. When we arrived home at 2:00 a.m., we took the elevator to the second floor. When the door opened, my wife could not walk out of the elevator. "I can't move," she said as the door closed. We just stood for five minutes waiting for her to get the strength to move forward.

The next night, we went out to dinner with friends. I mention these two trips to illustrate that my wife was still capable of getting around. This is important to know because, shortly, she would be in the I.C.U ward at Jefferson Hospital.

She started to sleep a lot, only getting up to eat and use the bathroom. On Tuesday, November 25, I made the decision to seek help. I called one of my sons, who had worked at Jefferson Hospital, and he made arrangements for her to be seen by doctors that day.

I went across the street to the water park and they brought over a wheelchair and helped me get her down into my car. When I got to the hospital, they immediately began to test her lungs because she was having difficulty breathing. It didn't take long before they found emphysema in both lungs, which didn't surprise me at all.

My wife became very nervous and scared, but when they told her she was going to go home, her face brightened. They gave us a couple of prescriptions. It looked like we soon would be leaving for Ocean City. However, another doctor came on the scene and suggested that they give her one more test.

The results of that test were not good and the doctors said that she could go home on Saturday, which was a four-day stay. They assigned her a room and she sort of accepted the fact that this was necessary. Little did she know that this was much more serious than even the doctors knew. It became a life-and-death situation much sooner than anyone could have predicted.

I came back the next morning and she was not in her room. The nurse told me that she had taken a turn for the worse during the night and was now in the intensive care unit. I was in shock. When I left the night before, she was sitting up and talking.

I went and sat in the waiting room, trying to summon up enough courage to go in and see her. The nurse told me that she had a breathing tube down her throat. The thought of seeing her suffering was just too much for me to face. It took me about one hour before I was brave enough to go in and see her.

We were 16 years old when we first met while attending Frankford High School in Philadelphia. I walked into a candy store across the street from the school and there she was, Catherine Barbara Reale – everyone called her "Cass." She was standing in line at the cash register. I had never seen her before that moment. We started to talk and we talked every day for the next 45 years. Little did either of us know that in four years we would be Mr. and Mrs. Paul? What would my life have been like if I hadn't walked into that candy store?

Now the big clock of life was counting down our time together. They had tortured her body and her mind for ten days. Her arms were twice their normal size from being stuck with so many needles. The breathing tube was still down her throat.

Nothing they tried seemed to work, so I met with the doctors and told them that if my wife was going to die, then I preferred that it be at our condo in Ocean City. They did not argue the fact that she wasn't responding to the treatments.

"She has suffered enough," I said to the doctors. They agreed to unhook her from all the hoses and machines that were keeping her alive.

On Friday night, December 5th at 7:00 p.m., we started our last journey to Ocean City. The ambulance arrived at the condo around 9:00 p.m. and they carried her up to it. When she was placed in her bed, she reached up and touched my face and smiled. It would be the last time that I would ever see her smile.

The clock of life was ticking even faster now. But at least she was home. The next day, Saturday, December 6th, 1997 at 9:00 p.m., she was watching television and seemed comfortable, but God was calling her. After a few gasps, it was over. It was 24 hours from her arrival home from the hospital.

She was gone from my life forever! Our time together had come to an end. It began in a candy store in Philadelphia and ended 80 miles away at our condo in Ocean City. In between the candy store and the condo were 45 years of memories that included raising three boys and one girl.

That was 12 years ago and those memories are starting to be very blurry. I try not to look back, but I just wish that somehow there would be a way to thank her for being the architect of this life that now consumes all my time and thoughts.

The human mind cannot accept the loss of someone who was with you day and night for 41 years. We can only try to get through each day with the help of God.

The architect of my life – Cass.
January 18, 1936 - December 6, 1997

—4—

A Fruitless Search

To say that my wife was different would be an understatement. Six months before we were to be married, I was informed that she wanted to invite her mother to our wedding in February. This may sound quite normal unless you knew that her mother had abandoned her when she was two years old.

The aunt and grandmother who raised Catherine advised her not to do it. Not a good idea, they said. She had her heart set on using our wedding to unite with her mother who had never, in eighteen years, attempted to contact her.

My wife knew her mother's first name was Clara, but she had to do some research to find out her last name, since she had remarried.

Amazingly, she found her and she lived only ten minutes from us. Now everything was in place for my wife's first meeting with her long lost mother.

It was about 7 o'clock on a warm August evening when we arrived at her mother's house. My future wife walked up and knocked on the door. She had a big smile on her face as she stood there hoping that someone would be answering. It was a very hard scene to write about.

I stood back about twenty feet. I don't know why, I just thought that it would be their moment and I was just a spectator. I could only imagine what was going through Catherine's mind.

Knock! Knock. The door opened and Catherine said, "Hi! I am your daughter!" It was stunning. The woman looked like Catherine's older sister. Their facial features were very similar. It was even more amazing that they did not hug or kiss.

I think that Clara could not believe that this reunion was happening.

We went inside and her husband was there. The conversation was very strained. It ended with an invitation to our wedding, which they accepted.

I wish that I could tell you that they lived happily ever after but her aunt and grandmother were correct about Clara. She had a new life with a husband and children; a twenty-year-old daughter from a previous marriage did not fit into Clara's plans. I know that you see and hear of all these heartwarming reunions but it didn't happen for Catherine.

My dear wife had played her last hand and now she knew it was best to move on. She never second-guessed her decision to find her mother. She got married, had four babies of her own and tried to be a good mom.

In hindsight, I wished at some point she would have kicked a few doors down or threw some dishes to get that monkey off of her back. Instead she carried it to her grave.

—5—
Why?

Why am I sitting on the beach? It is cold, windy and there is no sun. The answer: I am not sitting. I am actually running!

Running because I just lost my best friend, my high school sweetheart and my wife on the same day.

Running because I will be eating my breakfast, lunch and dinner by myself.

Running because I don't know if I can survive the death of my wife.

When I arose each morning, I noticed that my condo was getting smaller and smaller. The walls seemed to be closing in and the ceiling was dropping down. I knew that my sanity depended on how I handled these next few weeks.

When I arise in the morning, I will eat, wash, dress and be on the beach in 45 minutes. Why did I choose to run to the beach? Because when you get there, it is quite obvious that you can't run any farther. God drew a line in the sand for me and he wanted me to sit there until my mind could accept the loss of my wife.

"It will take time," he said. "But you will gradually get over Catherine's death, and you will begin a journey on this beach that will be beyond your wildest dreams. You and Catherine had a very special life together. But she is dead, and you are still alive. The beach will be your life and the ocean will calm your fears."

God was right. Even though the beach was my savior, it still took about four years before I was ready to turn the page. I then realized that, for the first time, I had full custody of my life. I had always compromised, but now I just did whatever made me happy.

If it was cold, windy, or even snowing, I just went to the beach. In the summertime, I went to the beach from 8 o'clock in the morning until it was dark. Soon I was spending hundreds of consecutive days and thousands of hours on the beach. I couldn't wait to get up in the morning and see what wondrous sights and sounds awaited me. The title of "King of the Beach" and "Number One Beach Bum" could be heard from my friends who were aware of my passion for the sand and ocean.

Naturally, because of the many days I spent on the beach, it entitled me to be classified as an expert on all activities "East of the Boardwalk." These include: beach etiquette, seagulls, bathing attire, sand, ocean, waves, tides, wind, boogie boarding, surfing, jellyfish, seaweed, beach umbrellas, lifeguards, etc.

The first two years, I did 360 days and the next two years I did 350 days. I knew that the weather could not chase me from the beach because I had worked for 41 years in construction. Being on the beach when it was cold and windy was just another day in paradise.

There was no doubt that I had become addicted to the beach but I never saw a sign that said, if you have a problem call 1-800-BEACH BUM.

Just another day in paradise...

—6—

Did You Ever...

Did You Ever...Get run over by a 600-pound waverunner?

I did! It was November 1995. My wife and I were just sitting around the condo on a cool, dark November afternoon so I told her I was going to go bodyboarding. She was not happy about my decision.

"You can't go down there by yourself. You will probably be the only one in the water," she said.

"What can happen?" I replied, as I pulled on my wet suit.

I grabbed my bodyboard and flippers and headed down to the beach. My wife's prediction was right – there was no one on the beach on this dark and gloomy afternoon. I waded out into deeper water, then jumped on my board and paddled out another 30 yards to wait for a wave. As I waited lying on my board, out of the corner of my eye, I saw something moving through the water. It was a wave runner!

He was headed towards me and, because I could clearly see him, I assumed that he could see me.

He was about 50 yards away, going about ten miles an hour and was quickly closing the gap between us. I lifted up my head and raised my arm, waving to him. Within seconds he was about to run me over. One bodyboarder, one person on a wave runner, in the big ocean and we were about to meet each other for the first and maybe the last. It was quite obvious that he had not seen me.

I was lying on my stomach so I grabbed the sides of my board and made a quick rolling motion, which put

my board between the 600-pound machine and me. I was almost on my back when I felt him making contact with my board. He tried to steer away from me and I somehow was able to muster up enough strength to actually push him off his wave runner. Sounds impossible but I know what happened.

He swam over to where we collided. "I didn't see you!" He said.

"That's quite obvious," I replied. I should have been really mad but I was just glad that I had no injuries.

Now I yell and shake my fist at any wave runner who gets within one hundred yards. These machines are just too big and fast for any man to say he can safely operate this missile safely around people or boats. There is no doubt in my mind that wave runners will slowly disappear from our waters because of the laws and regulations put on them by the state. Too big! Too fast! Too dangerous!

Did I tell my wife about my encounter? No way!

Did You Ever... Have a strange encounter on the beach?

July 2000, a good friend of mine owned a bed and breakfast located on the same street where I lived. One day he warned me that there was a very strange lady staying at his place and she surely would be heading to our beach.

Sure enough, this odd-looking woman appeared. She looked odd because it was mid-summer and she was wearing a dress on the beach. I watched her working her way across the sand trying to find someone who would talk with her. I tried to hide behind my newspaper, but there she was standing right in front of me.

She had a cigarette hanging from her lips and her mouth did not have a full set of teeth.

"Hello," she said as I put down my paper. "Do you live in Ocean City?"

"Yes," I answered, wondering how long she would be staying.

Next question: "Where did you live before Ocean City?" She was not going to be easy to get rid of.

"Philadelphia," I answered.

"Me, too," she said.

Next question: "Where did you go to high school?"

"Frankford High School," I replied.

"Me too," she said, and I got a feeling that all of her answers would be "Me too."

Her third question: "What year did you graduate?"

"June 1953," was my answer.

Sure enough, she said, "Me, too."

"This woman is some kind of nut," I thought. But then she started to mention people and things that only someone who went to Frankford would have known. I asked her name and she told me. I went back to my condo and found my yearbook and there she was, a beautiful blond girl who I remember seeing in some of my classes.

I never met her in those years at the high school, but 47 years later, I talked to her on the beach in Ocean City. I saw her at our 50-year reunion and she looked much better. What were the chances of her asking, "What high school did you go to?"

Did You Ever... See someone drown in the ocean?

I did. October 2002, on a bright, unusually hot day while sitting with my good friend, Heath Jenni. A man who looked to be about 40 years old started to enter into the ocean right where we were sitting. There were other people in the water because it was such a nice day and the ocean was still warm.

I knew from the previous day that there was a dangerous riptide moving from the south to the east. This was a very unusual current that happens only two or three times a year, but what was I to do – stand by the water and warn everyone? I tried this before, many times, with little success. People just have given me a dumb look and precede to go in anyway.

We watched him swim straight out into the fast-moving current, which was about a hundred yards from the beach. The poor man didn't feel the current until he turned around to come back. He was only able to swim ten yards when his arms started to wave for help.

His cries for help were heard and seen by my friend, Heath, who was young and in excellent shape. Heath grabbed my bodyboard and started paddling out. By now, the man had sunk under the water, so Heath started reaching down to grab him. He managed to pull him up by his hair and, with the help of another man, he managed to get him up onto the bodyboard.

The fire-rescue people arrived and a fireman with a rope swam out to join Heath. Because of the short time that he was under water, I hoped that he had survived.

He did not! The fireman continued to work on him for ten minutes, and then they took him to the hospital where he was pronounced dead.

There is a lesson to be learned here. Do not think that the ocean is a swimming pool. It is not! Just because you are a good swimmer and can easily swim a hundred yards does not mean that you will be able to do that in the ocean. The ocean is unforgiving and will usually win when tested. If you like to swim, just go out 20 yards then swim parallel to the beach it will be a lot safer.

Four other people have died while I was in the ocean bodyboarding. One of them was not found for four days.

He went in the ocean at Ninth Street and washed up just north of the Music Pier. It was kind of spooky to swim around knowing that you might bump into a body.

Did You Ever... Save a large Herring Gull from drowning?

I did in February 1999 while walking on the beach at 11th Street. I saw a seagull with his head down in the water about ten feet from the beach. I watched him bobbing his head up and down but never coming out of the water. Finally, after a short wait, his head shot up and, to my surprise, there was a large clam clamped down on the bird's bill. I thought he would eventually shake himself free but after watching him struggle for five minutes, it was obvious that the clam was winning this battle.

I knew that if I didn't soon help him, he would probably drown. So I ran three blocks back to my condo and put on a pair of high boots. Back I ran to the crime scene and I saw that things were the same. I waded out into the freezing cold water until I could reach out and grab the gull. I would need two hands to lift him; he was so big and heavy. His size and strength surprised me.

I reached down and grabbed the clam, which was about six inches in size, and with my free arm I wrapped it around the bird that was struggling wildly against me. I backed out of the ocean onto the beach.

Now I had a problem. How do I get the clam off of the seagull's bill? This had to be a strange sight with me

standing there with a clam in one hand and a seagull under my arm. Luckily, I saw a man walking towards me and he was not happy.

"What are you doing?" He asked. I turned and showed him the problem and he laughed.

"I was just going to punch you. I thought you were stealing a seagull," he told me.

We decided to use his car keys to crack open the shell of the clam. He wiggled the keys into the clam and soon we saw that the shell was starting to break. The bird was free and I released him into the air. He flew away, not even thanking me for saving his life. I only hope I'll get a few points for saving one of God's creatures.

Did You Ever... Get hypothermia?

I did twice!

I was now living at the shore year-round and it was easy for me to see that the surfers did not stop riding waves when the water became cold. This was great! Now I would stay in the ocean all year-round.

Someone had given me an old worn-out wet suit, so I was ready for cold-water fun. The problem was that nobody had ever explained to me the proper suit and accessories required to safely do it. I didn't even know what a safe water temperature was for the suit that I was wearing.

The water temperature that day was 38 degrees. But I just assumed that if I had a wet suit on with gloves and booties, I must be okay. The waves were fairly big that day, which required me to "duck-dive" under each wave going out. So now the 38-degree water was in my face and down into my suit. I found out that ducking my head into this cold water was not a good idea for a 60-year-old man.

I began to breathe heavily so I made the decision to get out. I started walking up the beach. I really didn't know where I was or why I was there. It felt like I was not going to make it back to our condo. The thought of my wife hearing an ambulance coming up our street pushed me to put one foot in front of the other. I was out of the water for almost ten minutes and I was still breathing like a hundred-yard-dash runner would after a race.

Finally my feet got me back to my condo and I walked right past my wife into the bathroom.

"How was the water?" she asked.

"Not bad!" I replied.

Not bad for a seal, is what I wanted to say. I got in the shower and let the hot water run down the back of my neck into my wet suit. I was surprised that I almost felt normal after only five minutes in the shower.

I never told my wife the true story of what happened that day and I didn't learn a lesson because I did it again a couple of years later. I learned to wear the proper wet suit and to avoid water lower than 45 degrees. I was able to bodyboard year-round until I was 73 years old and if you wear the right equipment, it is actually easier than you might think. Try it!

Did You Ever... See a whale while sitting on the beach in Ocean City?

I did, and many other people saw it, too. It was in June 1995. A whale (I don't know what kind) swam along our beach going up and down from 5th to 12th Street for about 13 days. The rails of the boardwalk were lined with people trying to get a glimpse of this 13-foot whale.

Did You Ever... See umbrellas fly fifty feet up into the air?

I did! It was a beautiful Sunday afternoon in July 1998. Out of nowhere, the wind started to blow. We always get these bursts of wind during the summer, but something seemed different about this wind that day. It started to swirl and, in 15 seconds, we were trapped in a violent whirling column of air.

There were about 25 large umbrellas in the area by the Music Pier and they started to pop out of the sand like they were parachutes, but they were going up, not down. I watched them as they climbed and it appeared that the umbrellas were almost as high as the Music Pier.

I looked around me to see what was happening on the ground and I saw a baby coach with a child in it start to lift. Fortunately, it ended as fast as it began. All of it took place in less than one minute but it is something the people on the beach will never forget.

When I told a couple of my friends that I would be writing a book about the beach, both of them said, "Don't forget to write about that wind swirl we were in that day on the beach."

Did You Ever... See 200 sea nettles in the surf?

I did! They are supposed to be the second most dangerous thing in our ocean. Our beach was covered with these creatures that were only two inches in diameter and had tentacles about three inches long. It was in early October and fortunately, only a few people were in the water.

Unfortunately, one of those people was my six-year-old grandson who got stung around the knee area. He screamed for about 20 minutes until I found something in my beach bag that seemed to work. That was five years ago and he still can show you the scar.

They were there for three days and I never saw them before or after that time.

Did You Ever... See a strange animal on the beach?

It was a llama, which stands about seven feet tall and weighs around 300 pounds. It's from the mountains of South America. Quite a sight when you're just sitting on the beach reading your newspaper.

Did You Ever... Ride down a ten-foot wave?

I did, one time! When I got halfway down, I realized that the wave was in charge. Soon I would find myself in a washing machine that had my head, arms and legs all going in different directions. I'll never try that again believe me!

Did You Ever... Have an Ocean City policeman chase you off a Jetty while you were fishing?

I did! It was October of 2009 at 2:00 p.m.

Why me, officer?

I had fished there for 14 years along with a hundred other fishermen. To my knowledge, I am the only one to have experienced this problem.

Why me, officer?

Hundreds of people walk onto the Jetty every year. I'm the only one to have been removed. It was a sunny day and the ocean was calm. I have seen many people out on these Jetties during storms and they never got chased.

Why me, officer? I have survived two bouts with cancer and I'm 74 years old. Just let me fish.

Did You Ever... Want to write a book about all of the things you have seen or done while sitting on the beach?

I'd tell you everything, but I want it to be a family book!

What am I trying to say, so diplomatically is: there are six or seven stories that I cannot put into my book.

Yes, they happened on the beach and in the ocean during daylight hours. Hard to believe, but true.

I have always told my friends that if you sit on the beach long enough, you will see everything imaginable here. There's something about the salt air and water I guess.

Did You Ever... See a live seal on our beach?

I did! March 2008 at 2 o'clock p.m. He came ashore just north of the 7th Street Jetty. He wobbled up the beach then just sat there looking around. He made some barking sound, turned and headed back into the ocean.

I thought he was gone, but within minutes he wobbled up onto the 8th Street beach. By now the police had arrived and cleared all of us off of the beach. We were told that seals have a nasty bite that carried bacteria.

Soon the marine stranding station from Brigantine arrived and captured him with a large net. They told me that if he were in good health, they would release him back into the ocean a couple of miles out.

Did You Ever... See a complete, unbroken beautiful rainbow come out of the ocean directly in front of you and end in Atlantic City?

I did! It's been about four times. What a beautiful sight. If you weren't on the beach, then seeing the complete rainbow would not be possible.

Did You Ever... Have a policeman question you about being a street person?

I did! While sitting on the beach in December of 2009, about one o'clock in the afternoon an Ocean City Officer approached me on the beach. I was the only one there, so I knew he was coming to talk to me.

"Hello Officer," I said. He started to eye me in a strange way.

"Do you live in Ocean City?" He asked. "What are your address, telephone number and date of birth?"

I answered all of the above while he wrote on a small piece of paper in his hand.

When he finished writing, he looked at me and said, "About an hour ago, we got a call that there was a street person living on this beach."

It surprised me because I was clean-shaven, my hair was combed and there was no newspaper inside my shirt or shoes to keep me warm. Still, he was determined to paint me as this person.

The interrogation was about to begin.

"Why do you have three beach chairs?" He asked. That had to be the dumbest question ever asked on the beach.

I was shocked by the question, but I managed to stutter out, "If I am on the beach and two of my friends come down, then I will need three beach chairs."

He looked at me kind of funny and I started to sweat. What if there was a "two chair limit" ordinance in December! I always thought that if I sat on the beach all day, I would stay out of trouble. Now I could possibly be fined or sent to jail for being a street person and a serial beach chair abuser!

What could I do, tell him that one of the chairs was a coffee table? No! That might confirm his street person theory. What will my friends say when they see me on the front page of the *Ocean City Sentinel?*

Finally, The officer left, still not convinced that I was not the notorious street person.

You thought that I had an easy life going to the beach every day. It's not easy being me! Tomorrow, I'm only bringing TWO beach chairs!

Did You Ever... Believe that when you die, you'll wake up on a beach?

This is not good news for those people that don't like sand.

Did You Ever... See mountains of seaweed?

Not everything about our beaches is beautiful, or pleasant-smelling. Every once in a while, the dreaded sight and smell of something called seaweed appears. It can ruin your day on the beach and you might not get into the ocean.

Even if you could remember the worst case of seaweed you ever saw, it would not come close to what I witnessed during the fall of 2002. When I left the beach the night before, the beaches were clear. During the night, the seaweed came in like never before.

When I arrived the next day, there were mountains of seaweed. It was like walking through a giant maze.

In some places it was six feet high. This lasted from 7th Street Jetty down to 10th Street. It covered the entire width as well. I thought that it was an event that happened often, fortunately, it never occurred again.

Did You Ever... See someone get stung by a Portuguese Man of War?

I did! It was in Florida. You do not want to ever see it happen. I can't describe what I saw when a boy around ten years old got stung across his back.

Did You Ever... Find 100 perfect Whelk Shells on the beach?

I did! It was in March of 1999. I was taking a walk down the beach after a big winter storm. Around 11th Street, I saw a large area of beach covered with what appeared to be seaweed. As I got closer, I noticed that among the seaweed were many beautiful shells.

I quickly ran back to my condo and grabbed a large bag. There were many shells. They were big and heavy. I could only carry fifty. I didn't know that people went crazy when they found one, and I'd found fifty!

I gave most of them away to children in my neighborhood. I still have about twenty, which I show off on my deck. In fifteen years, this event has only happened once. How lucky was I?

Did You Ever... Get stung by a red Jellyfish?

I did! Only once right in the face while riding down a wave. It hurt for about 20 minutes. That's why people won't go into the ocean while they are around.

Did You Ever... Catch a shark with just a bodyboard?

I did! One day after a hurricane had passed Ocean City the water was extremely rough. I looked out into the ocean and saw the dorsal of a shark sticking up out of the water. He was caught in the fast moving current, which was pushing him toward the beach.

The shark was about four feet long and ten inches round. I never found out what kind of shark he was, but I know it wasn't a common sand shark.

I could see that he was not going to make it back into the ocean, so I waded into the water, armed only with my bodyboard. I circled around him and started pushing toward the beach. A large crowd started to gather around to see a real shark come out of the ocean.

After a couple of minutes, everyone told me to put him back in the ocean. We picked him up carefully and carried him back into the water. He managed to catch a rip current and quickly disappeared.

Did You Ever...

Wish that you could write a song or a poem about our beautiful sandy beaches and ocean? The words and music should flow from my brain but nothing happens.

Ride your bodyboard in the same wave with a porpoise? They are scary-big when you get close to them.

Have a tall, beautiful blonde stalk you on the beach? No? Neither did I!

See three Portuguese men of wars on our beach in Ocean City? Yes! It was after a hurricane and they had to travel all the way from Florida.

Watch the colors of our amazing sunsets while sitting on the beach? Red, orange, yellow and pink are just some of these beautiful colors. How does God do that?

Get stung by a white Jellyfish? I didn't! They don't sting.

See the full moon come up and out of the ocean like a slow-motion picture? Then turn your head and witness the sun setting in the west, signaling the end of its day? I have seen it many times but it usually only happens in October.

Have an F-16 fighter jet tip his wing to you while sitting on the beach?

Walk through the snow to bodyboard?

Bodyboard at night by using the light of a full moon? I like doing it. And so do the sharks.

Wish you could freeze those perfect moments that happen on the beach?

Put on a bathing suit 300 days in a row?

Shovel off the snow to sit on the beach?

Bodyboard on a foggy day? I did and came out of the water two blocks from where I went in.

Wish that the summer would never end? That is why Labor Day is the saddest day of the year.

See the full moon come up out of the ocean and the sunset at the same time? I have, many times.

Sit on the beach with a cup of coffee before anyone else arrives?

Stay on the beach until you were the last one to leave?

Wish that the day on the beach would never end? Only 360 times a year!

Want to write a book all about the beach and only the beach? I'm going to try. Got to find a pencil.

Have your morning coffee with a pigeon? They come whether you invite them or not.

Bring four grandkids to Ocean City 25 weekends in a row? I did, many times. Just build yourself up with steroids before school gets out.

Thank God for a nice day on the beach?

Amen!

—7—

Wonder...

Wonder why God gave us seagulls, flies, gnats, jellyfish, and seaweed? I think he is testing all of us for patience and pain.

Wonder why people go to the beach to get some fresh, clean air and then smoke? Am I missing something here?

Wonder why children can have so much fun and be so happy when they come to the beach? They like it so much they cry when it's time to leave. So do I!

Wonder if bikinis can really get smaller? They come in small, tiny and go get a cop!

—8—

Lifeguards

Everyone will agree that lifeguards are very important people on our beaches. Yes, safety is a very important reason to respect our young men, and sometimes women, for the job they do so well. But they also dictate what kind of beach we will have that summer. If we have lifeguards who like to do their jobs and have fun, then we will have a fun beach.

Fortunately, our beach has been blessed with young men who enjoy what they are doing and are wonderfully patient when pestered by the young kids. Since they keep me from drowning every summer, it wouldn't be wise for me to criticize their performance as lifeguards.

I will save my negative comments for the female lifeguards who sometimes grace our beach. I do not know any of these mermaids, so this is not a gender thing. I spend a lot of time bodyboarding during the summer months and so do my grandkids. So God forbid that any of us would get into trouble on a big-wave day.

I want the biggest, strongest, and fastest lifeguards heading out to help us, not one of these tiny 100-pound females I have seen sitting at our lifeguard stands. It is not just me. Many people have raised this issue, wondering if the city couldn't find males who were bigger, stronger and faster. Sorry ladies, this is just about safety.

Lifeguards love what they are doing and pray for an endless summer, or moving Labor Day to October. I have spend a lot of time watching them and my expert opinions have been put into percentages which even some lifeguards have sanctioned. You should know I have interviewed multiple lifeguards in order to make this list.

They said it, not me:

10% of lifeguards would do their job for free.

10% would work for just food.

30% of lifeguards have never held a real job.

30% of lifeguards are not looking for a real job.

50% of the lifeguards would do their job for

50% of what they are now paid.

50% of the lifeguards like to blow their whistles 50 times a day.

60% of the lifeguards would quit if they couldn't talk with females.

80% of the girls who talk to the lifeguards wouldn't give them a second look at the mall.

60% of the lifeguards wouldn't give the girls who talk to them a second look if they saw them with clothes on.

30% of guys sitting on the beach would give their right arm to be a lifeguard.

70% of the girls with guys on the beach wish that their boyfriends were lifeguards.

100% of the lifeguards will never forget that being a lifeguard was and always will be the best job they ever had.

—9—

When I Am the Mayor...

It is the first week of July. The air temperature is 85 degrees. The ocean temperature is 72 degrees. It is 4:45 p.m. and the lifeguards start blowing their whistles to summon the people out of the ocean.

We are leaving the beach at 5 o'clock. I don't recommend that you swim without lifeguards on duty.

What! This is the world's favorite family resort and the day is over at 5 o'clock? There are still four hours of daylight left and you can't do what you came to Ocean City to do: swim in the ocean? This has got to change.

When I am the mayor, our beaches will be open from 10 a.m. until 7 p.m. during the months of July and

August. I have seen the lifeguards leave the beach with a hundred people still in the ocean. This is unconscionable. The only reason people don't drown is just pure luck and the grace of God. Yes, it will cost more but we all know that you can't put a price on safety.

When I am Mayor...

I will set aside the first Sunday in August as "Lifeguard Appreciation Day" in Ocean City. People who go to the beach regularly will surely know the lifeguards on the beaches by that time and they can show their appreciation for the safety lifeguards provide for our families. Gift cards, a meal at any restaurant in Ocean City, pizzas or just a nice thank-you will do.

Lifeguards really care about what the people are thinking while they are on duty. Here is your chance to show them.

—10—

Beach Wear

Recently, a friend gave me a book about the history of Atlantic City. I came across a page with a photo of women wearing bathing suits that covered them from head to toe. Beneath the picture, was a description of what it was like to go on the beach in the 1930s.

It said that men and women must be attired in appropriate swimwear, which must cover all parts of their bodies. The city employed beach censors to ensure that excessive skin was not exposed.

Wow! Have we come a long way since those days?

How did we ever get from no skin showing to the present-day custom of all skin showing? Why did so many girls and women decide that the beach was the proper place to display areas of their bodies that formerly were exhibited only in their bedrooms at home?

Modesty has been replaced with, "Hey, look at me". Material has been replaced with skin and flesh. Comfort has been replaced with 50 adjustments of the bikinis per hour.

There are even girls from ten to thirteen wearing these outrageous bikinis on the beach. Moms and Dads, what are you thinking about when you allow your young daughters to dress like they are eighteen? Let's start showing some "tough love." These young girls are not women. Buy them a one-piece swimsuit and say, "wear this or stay home."

Pardon the pun but I wish that I could get to the bottom of this question of why females like to expose themselves to everyone and anyone.

I would like to ask every female on the beach who is wearing one of these go-go outfits: why? They would probably call a cop or lie about their motives for disrobing in a public place.

They are certainly not built for comfort. Just watch the females walking down the beach. You will notice that they cannot walk five steps without adjusting their bikinis. Even when they are sitting on the sand or lying on a towel, every time they move, they must readjust their top and bottom.

You will also notice that they don't venture out into the ocean too often. Because they know that Mr. Ocean is waiting to strip them of their self-respect and dignity.

All of these problems could be overcome with a one-piece swimsuit. However, they fear that no male would ever look at them again. This is how they think, so we shall see more and more of these handkerchiefs which will get smaller and smaller.

The girls are uncomfortable, they have to continually fix themselves and they can't go into the ocean. They cannot really enjoy themselves. But this is a sacrifice that they are willing to make for the bikini gods.

There is no answer to this issue because it is about morals. These females would go nude if the police would let them so they just try to push the rule as far as they can. There is no doubt that someday Ocean City will have to employ beach censors just like they did in Atlantic City in 1930.

How about the overweight girls and women who think they can wear a bikini? They supply us men with hours of conversation and laughs. The good thing about it is that you will know what to buy these hefty babes for their birthdays – a mirror!

There definitely has been an increase in the number of large females wearing bikinis. I think that is related to the increase in ice cream, pizza and French fry shops on the boardwalk.

I know something about women's beachwear that I want to share with everyone.

When females come to the beach, they always wear what is called a "cover-up," which is actually a very short dress that fits over their bathing suit.

When they arrive on the beach, they remove it and proceed to prance around the beach all day with no problem. At the end of the day, when they know that they have to walk a hundred yards to their condo, the "cover-up" is put back on.

Apparently, women have come to the conclusion that all the "dirty old men" are only on the west side of the boardwalk. This is really great police work on the ladies' part and I will inform the Ocean City police of their findings.

Now that I have savaged female beach wear, it is only appropriate that I dismantle the men's attire. Keep in mind that I am an expert on everything on the beach. If I say that something isn't right, you must remember that this came about only after months of observation of males on our beaches.

Whoever told these boys and men they looked good or cool in bathing suits that go down to their knees or lower? The women are wearing less and the men have been adding material on.

If these males could find a pocketbook and high heels, they would look like babes. Don't they look at pictures of themselves? Whoever told them that they look masculine wearing those short dresses?

Men, start showing off your legs! You still will be showing only 25% of what the females show. Buy swimsuits with six-inch seams that will allow you to show off your muscular thighs. The ladies will start giving you a second look when they see your rippling muscles as you walk on the beach.

Get rid of the dresses and start to look like a man. You are wearing these skirts because everybody else is wearing them, not because you look good. You will be forever grateful that I brought this to your attention.

You will also find out that the shorter bathing suits are more comfortable and the chances of getting rashes on your legs will be reduced. I know that this is a true because my friends are constantly borrowing my rash guard gel. Doesn't make sense to me – buy six-inch seam bathing suits and fight the females off.

—11—
Birds of My Beach

It sounds strange but I spend more time on the beach with birds than I do with people. Once October comes, the beaches empty and it is just sparrows, laughing gulls, red bill gulls, pigeons and I. This has allowed me to become an expert on their everyday habits and strange behavior.

I have studied these birds for years and, believe it or not, they have been studying me too. They watch everything I do and this is because I represent a possible source of some food. These birds are about food and nothing but food. From morning to night, it is about finding something to fill their stomachs.

Do I feed the seagulls? No! Do I feed one or two of them? Yes. I know that Ocean City has passed laws about feeding seagulls, but council members don't come to the beach every day like I do or they would see that the seagulls are running out of food, probably because of beach replenishment. In the last five years, clams, crabs, minnows, jellyfish and seaweed have almost disappeared. I watch the seagulls for hours eating nothing, so that is why I became a person of interest for them.

You do not need laws to stop people from feeding the gulls in the summertime. The problem is always handled on the beach in two ways.

1. The local residents who are sitting near the shoobies feeding the gulls will give these people a look that would stop a train

2. The shoobies will quickly find out that they can't just feed a couple of gulls. In a matter of seconds, an army of hungry gulls will attack the shoobies. Case closed!

* * *

The most remarkable bird on our beach is the laughing gull. He is the smallest of all the gulls and is recognizable by his black head and screeching voice that can be used instead of water boarding to make people crazy. This gull is cunning, calculating, carefree and annoying.

He arrives in Ocean City around the second week in April. You can tell when he arrives because you will hear the police sirens. They will leave on the second week of October and you will hear church bells ringing. His eyesight is unbelievable. He can spot a crumb at a hundred feet, swoop down and identify in a split second if it is edible or not.

Everyone hates them because of their stealthy way of snatching food from your hand or mouth. They sit or fly in back of you, knowing that the French fries you have were brought for them. Their aim and timing is a work of art that is successful most of the time. Adults will cuss and throw things at them. Young children become frightened or even injured by their sharp bills.

Three laughing gulls were on the beach sharing a lunch from Mack and Manco's and a large red bill charged at the three smaller gulls and stole their pizza. The laughing gulls took off and the big gull thought that he would settle down to a nice meal, but the laughing gulls returned, swooping down north and south, brushing the red bill's head each time. After four bombing runs, the big guy decided to give the laughing gulls the pizza. That is why I called them calculating.

I once taught a laughing gull to sit on my leg while I was sitting in my beach chair. They are easy to train with food but be careful – they are not toilet trained.

They work very hard to ruin your day by stealing your food, which is why their nickname is "the flying rat." I heard that the rats were not at all happy about this comparison.

There are other seagulls on our beaches that most vacationers seldom notice. They are called herring gulls and some do stay around for the summer, but most of them don't arrive on our beaches until October and they will leave by May.

They are twice as big as the laughing gulls but, fortunately, the herring gulls are not as aggressive. That doesn't mean they won't steal food from your blanket. I once saw one of them pull dollar bills from a woman's pocketbook and the wind took them down the beach.

It is funny that you can leave your valuables on the blanket and go for a dip in the ocean and usually your things are safe. But if you do the same with food, the herring gulls will invade and wipe you out.

Conclusion: good people, bad seagulls. Herring gulls are famous for dining out at our trash cans. Their specialty is pulling pizza boxes out onto the beach. They know from years of experience that this is their best chance for acquiring a good meal. But what a mess they leave! The city should empty these trash cans at the end of every day. If they would come to the beach and see it for themselves, it would be a no-brainer.

If there are 20 herring gulls on the beach, usually the oldest and the biggest will be the dominant one. He will try to intimidate any smaller bird that just happens to walk too close to him or something he's looking at. He will rush at his victim and try to grab him by the feathers. Sometimes, they will pick on a young aggressive gull and find themselves in a real battle, which seldom results in serious injuries.

Pigeons are a beach bird. You heard it here first. I know that this is true because they will pester me all winter. They are easily the most intelligent bird on the beach and humans do not frighten them at all. You can chase them, throw sand at them and they will just move far enough away to discourage your actions and then come right back into your area just to show you they can.

The problem with pigeons is that they think that they are part of the human race. I have seen them sit between my friends and listen to everything we are saying. They close their eyes to take a nap and give you a strange look like you're talking too loud. You can't be too friendly with them because then they think that you should share whatever you are eating.

They are always ready to fight other pigeons or seagulls if pushed. They will even give their wives a good smack with their wing if it will get them the major share of any food.

I have a saying. "If you feed one pigeon, it will be fun. If you feed two pigeons, it will be interesting. If you try to feed three or more, watch out!"

You can bet that one of them will fly back to his hangout and alert all of his relatives that there is food on the beach. He will come back with the whole family.

Pigeons are usually round and fat, which make them a real target for hawks. Pigeons are very aware of this and will explode into flight if there is anything flying above their heads. When they do this, it is also a signal to all pigeons in the area to take flight. They do not wait around for someone to tell them that a hawk is in the area. "Fly now, ask questions later" is their motto. A lot of pigeons must get eaten for them to be so squeamish.

One other bird is not thought to be one of our beach birds and that is the tiny brown sparrow. He makes his home in the long grass and bushes on our dunes. Sparrows are my favorite bird on the beach because they act so normal. They have a family structure, very seldom fight, and share their food.

I feed them birdseed and it is almost impossible to fill them up. Some mornings, I forget to bring down their food and they will all sit in front of me looking like lost sheep until they shame me into going back to my condo.

In the summertime, they, like the rest of the birds, get their food supply from the boardwalk. They are still living in the dunes, so when there is a shortage of food, they will look me up out on the beach. My friends will swear that what I say is true. Even though there are five hundred people and one hundred umbrellas, they will find me on the beach.

They will leave the beach when the real cold or snow arrives. They try to find places near houses that have heat or just somewhere out of the weather. I miss them until they return in April.

—12—

Bodyboarding

Do you want to add five to ten years to your life? Then let me tell you how I was able to accomplish this amazing feat.

Sometime in the late 1980s, my wife and I were spending the weekend on DeLancy Street in Ocean City. It was a nice sunny day and we were enjoying ourselves with our friends who owned a house on the beach block. We didn't have to go too far to sit, because the high tide was up under the boardwalk, so we proceeded to place our chairs down in the "street."

It was a strange sight to see people sitting in the street and it was not hard for us to decide on finding another place on the Jersey coast. To top it off, when we went to our car, the Ocean City police had given us a parking ticket because our car was one foot over the yellow paint on the curb. Good-bye Ocean City!

We picked out a barrier island north of Atlantic City, which is where my wife's father happened to live. Just by chance, we went to a beach that was only for surfing. This kind of event was always occurring in my life. Why did we wind up at a surfing beach?

We put all our "stuff" down and enjoyed having a beach with a lot of white sand under our feet. It was better than asphalt! When it came time for me to go swimming in the ocean, I found that I would have to walk a hundred yards north of where we were sitting. It was a surfing beach only!

There were two people with what they called "bodyboards" in the water with the surfers. On our next trip down, my wife saw a surf shop on the main street going into Brigantine.

"Stop!" my wife shouted; "There's a surf shop! Go in and buy a bodyboard and you won't have to leave our beach to swim."

The board cost forty dollars, which seemed at the time to be a lot of money for something just to float on. If my wife weren't so smart, I would have had a very dull life.

I struggled to learn how to be a good bodyboarder but, because it was comparatively new, I didn't have anyone to instruct me on how to catch and ride a wave. All I knew was it was exciting and fun to do. I couldn't wait for the next week to come to try it again.

When you are in the learning stage of anything, you will make mistakes. One foggy day I went in to ride some waves. I was out there about thirty minutes riding waves and I couldn't even see the beach. I started to tire so I rode a wave in.

When I got onto the beach, I didn't know where I was! I didn't see my wife, so I started walking up the beach. It was hard to believe that I had drifted almost two city blocks. I found my wife, but I never told her what I had done.

When the water started to get cooler in September, my thoughtful wife decided that I needed a wet suit so I could continue to go bodyboarding. We stopped at the surf shop and I purchased something that I knew nothing about – a "Shorty " black wet suit. We headed to the beach and I couldn't wait to try out my new "toy."

I put it on and headed into the ocean. I was enjoying my first dip wearing a wet suit when I looked up and saw a man talking to my wife on the beach. I saw him point at me and I just thought that he was admiring my bodyboarding. He started to walk towards me and he motioned for me to come out of the water.

"He just wanted some bodyboarding advice," I thought.

"How long have you been bodyboarding?" he asked.

"Oh, about two months," I replied. "Why?"

"Well, did you know you put your wet suit on backwards?"

How embarrassing was that? How was I to know that the zipper went in the back?

I did a lot of bodyboarding over the years, and I found it to be just as addictive as smoking or drinking. If you ride one hundred waves in a day, you want to ride one hundred one. The thrill of riding down a big wave cannot be matched by the best ride at an amusement park.

And so now I can get back to my beginning question. Do you want to add five to ten years to your life? There is a way to make it happen and that is to start bodyboarding. I discussed this point with my bodyboarding friends and I wanted to say five, but they all said ten years.

Like all good things that will make your life better, it is not for everyone. The most important thing is you must live near an ocean because, if you don't do it often, then the guarantee of a longer life span will not be possible. This is at least a three times a week, eight months out of the year proposition. You might say that going to the gym will do the same thing, but the big difference is that bodyboarding is "fun" while the gym can feel like going to work.

While you are having fun, your arms and legs will get stronger and your stomach will get flatter. Getting used to the flippers on your feet will take time but most people adapt to them in one or two weeks. It is very important that you select flippers that fit you properly when you buy them. If they don't feel right, try another pair.

Once you make the decision to be a bodyboarder, be sure that you are in good health. I have seen older people try it for the first time and it was scary. They were completely out of breath and turning blue. I thought that I was going to be calling 911.

A friend of mine on the beach wanted to become a bodyboarder. He was in his forties and he felt that, because he still played soccer, he must be in good shape. He took my board and went out into the ocean for his first lesson. After twenty minutes of trying to catch a wave, he retreated to the beach.

"I see what you mean!" he said. "It's a lot harder than I thought."

I started my bodyboarding career at the ripe old age of fifty, which means that I have been doing it for over twenty years. So don't let age stop you from getting started in this wonderful water sport. Just make sure your heart is ready and able to handle "Mister Ocean." He can be a very intimidating and unforgiving monster at times, but you will love and respect him, as you start your journey to adding years to your life!

A few of my grandchildren – Plymouth Place Posse: Ryan, Kevin, Nicholas and Emily Dayton.

—13—

It's *About* the Beach

It is *astonishing* to see children scream and cry when their parents try to get them to walk on the sand.

It makes me *mad* when I see a seagull swoop down and snatch food out of a child's hand.

It is not *fair* when a family waits all year for their vacation in Ocean City and it rains four days in a row.

It was *funny* to hear that one of my friends thought that I was a homeless person, because he always saw me on the beach.

It is *amazing* how many people pick up small pieces of shells on the beach and act like they found a piece of gold.

It's hard to *believe* that the number one activity on the beach is taking pictures with a cell phone.

It *frightens* me when I see 15-foot waves heading for the beach.

It *sickens* me when people leave their trash on the beach.

It is *laughable* when the people lying on the beach think that the ocean is going to stop right before their blanket.

It is *inspiring* to see a group of dolphins riding in the waves.

It is *disgusting* when a seagull craps in your hair.

It is *wonderful* to lay with your bare back on the hot sand.

It is *heaven* when the ocean water temperature rises to 75 degrees.

It is amazing that people look *doubtful* when you tell them that sand kills more people than the ocean does.

It *brings a tear* to my eye when I see a young child run down to touch the ocean for the first time.

It makes me *sad* when I see an old man sitting on the beach in a wheel chair. He remembers when he was young.

It makes me *smile* when the ocean rushes up the beach and wets the shoes and socks of the unsuspecting visitors.

It makes me *wonder* when they just stand there and get hit with another wave from Mr. Ocean.

—14—
Beach Bum?

My friends and I spend countless hours sitting in the hot sun, fighting winds of 20 miles an hour which covers us with sand. We are on the beach from eight o'clock in the morning until eight o'clock at night. We have to get there early so as to get our "spot" on the beach.

If our expert surveyor misses the high tide location by ten or twenty feet, we will be shoveling sand for one to two hours because there is no place to move to on our crowded beach. This will exhaust the young and the old, but it is an exercise that keeps a lot of us in excellent shape.

When a thunderstorm approaches, beach bums must be the last ones to leave the beach and the first ones to return when the storm has passed. When it comes time to call it a day, you cannot leave the beach while it is still light. If you do, then you wrapped up too early. Finding your "stuff" in the dark is just part of the fun of being beach bums.

This is why my blood boils when I hear someone tell me that they are beach bums or their family and friends are beach bums. To call some of these people beach bums is disrespectful to all the people who have made so many sacrifices to prove their addiction, obsession and love for our beaches. Here are a few things that will eliminate people from beach bum status:

Arriving on the beach after 11 a.m.

Leaving the beach before 7 p.m.

Missing a day on the beach to go to the Cape May Zoo

Leaving the beach to catch the "early bird special"

Going to the movies on a sunny day

Not going to the beach on a windy day

Failure to go to the beach because it is hot or cold

Leaving the beach because there are flies or gnats

Not knowing what a tide is

Running back to your condo for a five o'clock dinner

Anyone young or old can become a beach bum. All it takes is a total commitment to the ocean and sand gods. You must allow yourself to be seduced by the sun, sand and water until their magical beauty overcomes your ability to do anything except being a beach bum.

Warning! It is addictive and you will suffer through deep depression when Labor Day comes. But you will survive, and all of those memories that you have stored in your brain will make you smile all winter long.

Please don't use work and kids as an excuse to keep you from coming aboard. Most of my beach bum friends work and have kids. The kids will sign up right away because they do not like to leave the beach at the best time of the day. Mom and Dad will at first find it hard to spend all day on the beach, but they will adjust their schedules when they realize that every day seems like the 4th of July.

You must first forget about wrapping up your stuff to run home and prepare dinner. A four- course dinner awaits you on the beach. Starting with pizza followed by delicious French fries and washed down with a water ice. If the kids eat all of their dinner, treat them to Kohr Brothers' ice cream.

When dinner is over, just sit there and watch everyone leaving while there are still three hours left of playing and talking with your fellow beach bums. This is the only way that you can slow up the summer. The beach bums have tried to slow it up by spending more time on the beach. More sand, more hours of sun and family. We can't stop the endless summer from rushing to the finish line but it "shore" will seem longer.

—15—

Beach Etiquette

Thousand of vacationers visit our beaches in Ocean City every summer. They have thought about their one-week vacation for almost a year. They will arrive with their dreams of spending many hours sunning themselves on our sandy beaches.

Hopefully they will realize their dream and return home with many fond memories of happy days on the beach in Ocean City. I am here 52 weeks every year so I just wait for the annoying people to leave on Saturday, which is called "check-out day."

However, you are only here for one week, so we must

do something to assure everyone who visits Ocean City that we really care about the time you spend on our beaches.

I have spent many hours talking to friends, family and vacationers about their worst experiences. I listened to all their stories these last 14 years and put them together with all the problems I myself have witnessed. I have experienced firsthand many violations of what we call "beach etiquette."

I have always believed that when you purchase a beach tag, you should be issued a pamphlet explaining proper beach behavior. I know that it would be hard to enforce these rules and suggestions, but maybe people will realize that there are dos and don'ts on our beaches. Stupid things, rudeness, bad manners, bad language, etc. should be left back at your condo.

When I mention this idea to give pamphlets with each beach tag, every one of my friends say "great idea." So I thought of the most common issues discussed on the beach and compiled them into a list of rules, which should help our visitors take home fond memories of their vacation in Ocean City.

Rule #1: Do not sit "on top" of people when you arrive at the beach to set up your chairs, umbrellas, etc.

Assumption #1: "I can sleep until 10 am, go to breakfast, ride my bike and still sit in the same area as the people who arrive on the beach at 9 a.m." Wrong!

Common Sense #1: Be aware of how close you are to your neighbors when you set up your "stuff." Leave enough room so that people, coaches, wagons and wheelchairs can easily navigate to and from the beach. If you can't adjust your schedule in the morning to get on the beach, then you must locate in an area where you might not want to sit. Just don't make your problem my problem.

Rule #2: Know what the tide schedule is when you come to the beach. Understand how a tide comes in and out before you set up your "stuff."

Assumption #2: "I'll just go down and set up by the water and when the tide comes in, we'll just move our stuff back to where other people have been sitting. Everyone has to move back for us, right?" Wrong!

Common Sense # 2: Once again, you are making your problem everyone else's problem. Relocate, and educate yourself about how tides work. Six hours in, six hours out. Check your local morning paper for the times of high and low tides on our beach. This is a big problem on crowded beaches.

Rule #3: Parents, control your children. Know where they are, what they are doing and how much they are yelling. I know that you are on vacation but so is everyone around you.

Assumption #3: "My kids won't feed the seagulls!" "My kids won't throw sand!" "All the people sitting around me just love to hear my kids scream and whine all day."

Common Sense #3: Don't bury your face in a book. Don't talk on your cell phone. Don't read a newspaper. Watch your children! Everyone around you will appreciate it.

Rule #4: Only bring a radio to the beach if you are using earphones.

Assumption #4: "All the people sitting around me just love the music I am playing." Wrong!

Common Sense #4: Can't you leave your radio back at the condo? Sit back and listen to the beautiful sounds of the ocean.

Rule #5: If it is possible, don't bring your cell phone to the beach. If it is a necessity, keep your calls short and your voice at a low volume.

Assumption # 5: "Everyone around me loves to hear my cell phone ring 20 times a day." "Everyone likes to hear about the problems at my work place." "Everyone wants to hear how important I am." Wrong!

Common Sense #5: I don't care if your ring tone plays "God Bless America." It can get very annoying after ten calls. Put your cell phone on vibrate. I'm retired; I don't want to hear about your job all day. Just because your kids have cell phones, do they all have to call you every five minutes? The beach was a better place before cell phones.

Rule #6: Don't bring your cheap Wal-Mart umbrellas to our beaches. They can become a dangerous flying missile.

Assumption #6: All beach umbrellas will work at the beach. Wrong! Beach umbrellas have a point on the top and on the bottom. Many people are hit, stabbed, gouged and impaled while just sunning themselves.

Common Sense #6: Only bring umbrellas to the beaches that are well made and able to withstand strong gusts of wind, which often blow on a hot summer day. They should be at least equal to the umbrellas that are rented on our beaches. These umbrellas are proved to be sturdy and able to withstand strong gusts of wind. Notice that they are slanted into the wind and installed to a depth of at least 12 inches. It is embarrassing to have your umbrella fly out and strike a person

Rule #7: Do not sit down by the ocean to sun yourself, take a nap or read a book.

Assumption #7: "I know that the children playing down by the water will not splash me." Wrong! "If they dare to get water on me or my book, I will give their parents a nasty look. I am on my vacation so don't play near me!" Wrong!

Common Sense #7: You choose to sit in a children's play area and if you insist on sitting there, then you and your book are going to get wet.

Rule #8: Don't bring footballs, kites and Frisbees to the beach when it is crowded.

Assumption #8: "I know exactly where these flying toys are going to go or land." No, you don't!

Common Sense #8: Leave these harmful objects at home. We all will be a lot safer. There are many other ways to have fun.

Rule #9: Do not bring alcoholic drinks to the beach. This is a dry town.

Assumption #9: "No one will know I'm doing it." Wrong! I don't care how well you disguise the container; the smell will travel with the wind.

Common Sense #9: Can't you people go a couple of hours without a beer? If you can't, I have a 1-800 number for you to call. You know that you're breaking the law. Don't you care? This is why people choose Ocean City over other shore resorts. They are trying to get away from people like you. This is the greatest family resort for a good reason. Please find another Jersey resort next year.

Rule #10: Do not do anything that will force the lifeguards to blow their whistles.

Assumption #10: Everybody just loves to hear the lifeguards blow their whistles 50 times a day. It is music to their ears. Wrong!

Common Sense #10: We all can cut down on the amount of this annoying torture to our ears if we just obey some rules:

Try to swim between the green flags. People are either color blind or they like to bother the lifeguards.

Keep off the jetty. Can't you read the signs?

Do you have to be the furthest one out in the ocean?

When you see people being pulled out when there is a "rip" current, avoid that area of the ocean.

Rule #11: When you arrive on the beach to set up your "stuff," try not to use any more sand then you will need to be comfortable.

Assumption #11: "When I rented my condo, I thought that it came with a fifteen by fifteen foot area of sand." Wrong!

Common Sense #11: Unfortunately, there are no ordinances governing how much sand someone may use when they come to the beach. It would be easy for someone, or many people, to simply take over a large section of the beach. I saw a family come down to the beach and proceeded to rope off a large area. People complained to the lifeguards, who contacted their headquarters. They were told that there is no limit to how much space may be controlled by a person or group. But sometimes we all need to ask ourselves if we are occupying too much sand? Be considerate of others.

Rule #12: Leave the beach as clean as you found it.

Assumption #12: Ocean City provides maid service on the beach just like my mother does when I'm at home. I don't have to clean my condo when I leave.

Common Sense #12: You know the cans, bottles and trash that belong to you or your group. Put them in them in the proper trash containers when you leave the beach.

—16—

Bow Wow City

God made the spectacular mountains, the incredible rivers, lakes and streams. But he saved his best work for our beautiful sandy beaches. Which the "dog people" of Bow Wow City turned into their own private toilet! It is a shame that I have to bring God into this issue but I need all the help that I can get.

The dog people scurry past the lawns of their neighbors because they know that they are being watched. Safer territory awaits them on our beaches where hardly anyone cares that they will be crapping on "God's front lawn."

This is because city council passed an ordinance that has no teeth. They never thought of how the dog laws of our city would be enforced. There are no police watching them day and night as the dogs run free and not only pollute our beaches but scare people who just want to enjoy a walk on the beach.

Since there is no one around to watch these law-breakers, the problem goes on and on day and night. And it will go on and on until the people of Ocean City demand that dogs not be allowed on our beaches, period!

I think that council or the police can stop these dog people from doing whatever makes "Lassie" happy is like believing in the Tooth Fairy. Their dog's happiness comes first and you can stick the laws in your ear. They are very aware of our dog laws but they also know that Bow Wow City does not have the people or the motivation to even stop them.

For this reason, after 15 years of trying to keep "my

beach" safe and clean, I have decided to throw in the towel. I am tired of dealing with these crazy dog people who have many times tried to do me bodily harm. The police have presented more problems than it has solved for me. The police really do not want to do it, and their clever demeanor always made me feel uncomfortable.

The problem was that they never understood how threatening and out of control the dog people are, even though my phone calls to them described the frightening actions of my tormentors. When I told these law-breakers that they had to put their animals on a leash or they had to clean up their mess, it was World War III. They would start to "freak" and make threats to harm me. "I'm going to kick your ass. I'm going to have people take care of you. I'll find out where you live." These were just a few of their favorite threats.

One lady actually took a swing at me, which just glazed my chin, while 50 people looked on. Twice I had to ask the police for immediate response. The person was so out of control, these people are really scary. A big dog without a leash approached me one day so I grabbed a shovel to protect myself.

I told the lady, "If you don't put the dog on a leash, then I will have to call the police."

"If you call the police, I'll tell them that you hit me with the shovel," she responded. This is what I have to deal with every day, council!

Dog owners run their dogs on the beach because they don't have to clean up when the dog craps. They just pretend that they didn't see them doing it. Why do you think that people walk their dogs on the beach at night? Same reason, "can't see what my dog is doing – it's too dark."

Even when they see the dog do it, they simply bury it in the sand. City council, do you want your children and grandchildren to dig and play in that sand? It is loaded with dangerous bacteria capable of making anyone who touches it deathly ill. Keep in mind that a hundred percent of the people who run their dogs without a leash do not clean up the dog excrement from our beautiful beaches.

Here are a few statistics that city council should be aware of: 800,000 people are bitten each year, just in the United States. Also, there are 800,000 people who say that their dog would never bite anyone and 370,000 of these bites require hospital treatment.

Does a person or a child have to be seriously hurt or disfigured before we realize that dogs must be completely removed from the beaches? Forget about the signs… dog people can't read English. Just go up on our boardwalk and see "no dog" signs on every block. We must learn a lesson about dog people.

—17—

Bow Wow City: Conclusion

Many years ago, the dog people of Bow Wow City pressured the mayor and city council to allow dogs onto our beaches. Council caved in, not caring or realizing that they were opening "Pandora's Box" that will be very hard to close.

Council passed some laws that just wasted time and paper. They also employed a part-time "dog catcher" forgetting that there are 24 hours in a day. Now we have dogs running free and doing their business regularly on our beaches.

If I could go back in time and be a council member,

this is what I would have said to the dog people: When you were thinking about getting a dog, did you contact city council? Did you contact the police? No! You made the decision to take on the responsibility of owning a dog. And it is a great responsibility, isn't it? After you got the dog, you found out that your neighbors liked their beautiful front lawns as much as you did. So now you have a problem, which you want to be our problem. You want it to be a problem for the police. You want it to be a problem for our citizens who like to sit or walk on our beaches. Our children and grandchildren will be exposed to your dog's feces, which even if you clean it up, will still leave dangerous bacteria in the sand.

This, of course, is hindsight, which is always 20/20, and I fully realize that council members do not have the time to sit all day on the beach like I do. But I wish that council would see the beaches though my eyes. I have given you a video of what goes on every day. If you believe the picture, then you must act. If you don't believe it, then get a beach chair and see for yourself!

The beaches of our great city are our most precious assets, even more important than the boardwalk. Without the beaches, there would be no boardwalk. It is impossible to say dog and beautiful beaches in the same sentence. Unless it says "Welcome to the beautiful beaches of Ocean City, which are dog-free."

With grandkids David and Jackie Paul.

—18—

Why Dogs Must Be Banned from Our Beautiful Beaches

Dog poop is not just unsightly; it's also a potential temptation to dogs that have an affinity towards it – as disgusting as that sounds.

The environmental protection agency has classified dog poop as a dangerous pollutant. That means dog poop is as toxic as certain chemicals and oils; and that's a not just folks jumping on the "green" bandwagon. That classification was made 20 years ago.

The US Center for Disease Control and Prevention has confirmed that dog poop can spread parasites – including salmonella, tapeworms and hookworms. If you don't believe it, just leave your dog's poop on your lawn for a few days and see how many parasites crawl all over it. And those parasites won't just disappear when the poop does; eggs from the parasites will linger for years – yes, years! If you or your dog comes in contact with the soil, there is a risk of infection from the parasite eggs.

Do you know that un-scooped poop from the beach can be washed into the ocean? Do you really want to be responsible for contaminating our ocean?

Dog poop is a team player and likes to get together with harmful bacteria like E. coli and fecal coli and form bacteria, which can cause intestinal illness including cramps and diarrhea and even kidney disorders.

Last, and certainly not least, dog poop can cause blindness in humans! How does that happen? The roundworm larvae can migrate through the body causing disease to the kidneys, liver, brain, lungs, eyes and heart. If adults or children touch the infected sand, they can become infected.

Get the dogs off of our beautiful beaches!

—19—
Someday Maybe...

They will find the technology needed to halt the loss of sand from our beaches after a storm. Beach replenishment is not the answer. The first year is wonderful. The second year is okay and the third year is a disaster. We must break this cycle.

The city will find it in their heart to give all the year-round residents of Ocean City free beach passes. It is embarrassing to pay to go on our beaches. It's like paying to play in your own back yard.

We will have ramps, and not steps at each and every beach entrance. The handicap laws were passed many years ago, but people in wheelchairs and babies in coaches must struggle to get on and off of our beaches. When will the city finally realize that the beaches are our number one priority?

I will live long enough to enjoy the effects of global warming on our cold winter beaches.

There will be showers located at every beach exit so that we don't carry the sand back to our cars, condos and houses.

Smoking will be prohibited on our beaches. Let them walk up to the boardwalk and use the areas marked out for smoking. Most of them probably couldn't walk that far because they smoke.

Someday, maybe Ocean City will become a leader instead of a follower. There will be showers at every exit, ramps instead of steps, and no smoking and free beach tags. Will this happen in my lifetime? I doubt it.

—20—

Top Ten Reasons
Why I Am Always on the Beach

#10   The seagulls wouldn't have anyone to annoy.

#9   The price to sit there is reasonable.

#8   If you're good at doing nothing, there isn't a better place to be.

#7   The city has me wired to the Tsunami early warning system.

#6   Beach bum is the only job you can have that you can be called a bum and it is a compliment.

#5 I still think the world is flat and I enjoy seeing the boats go over the edge.

#4 I am making sure the tide goes in and out every day.

#3 I am watching the boats out on the ocean. My financial advisor told me that someday my ship would come in.

#2 I enjoy doing nothing. Will somebody please tell me when I am finished?

#1 If I don't show up every day, my friends will think that they're on the wrong beach.

—21—

I Give Up

Day after day, I sit here looking for words that would properly describe the sun shining down on the blue ocean. Sometimes I think that I have found those words but when I try to shout them out or write them down, nothing appropriate matches this magical display.

Sun glitter, sun dust, diamond chips and star shower all sound nice but really do not capture the beauty of this spectacle that is performed on a sunny day. I feel that we will just have to make up new words since the ones we know and speak do not reach the highest levels of my mind. How will I ever write a poem or a song if I can't finish it because of the failure of scholars and dictionaries? Haven't these people ever sat here and watched the sun dancing on the ocean? I'm waiting for an answer. Frankly, I give up!

—22—

Lucky

I am so lucky to have found a new life in this wonderful city. There are many nice people and just a few clunkers. People who were born and raised in Ocean City are the luckiest people in the world.

When my wife passed away in 1997, I decided to run to the serenity of the beaches. When I would arise in the morning, 45 minutes was all I needed to find my feet resting in the sand. Now 14 years later, I am still doing the same thing.

I know it must seem strange to a lot of people, but all the people who tell me they envy my lifestyle easily balance their opinion.

The lifetime residents of Ocean City will always regard me as just another shoobie from Philly, but that's okay. I would like to thank them for letting me use their beaches to become the biggest beach bum in the history of Ocean City.

—23—

Sun of Mine

Well, Earl, old buddy – it's time to say goodbye for another day. I have a real nice sunset planned for you. I'm going to do the yellow and orange that you like so much. I cannot understand why more people don't come down to the beach and see my sunsets. I try to produce a masterpiece every day but you are the only one I can count on to watch them. I saw you with some friends a couple of days ago and they did not look impressed at all.

It was pink, orange and yellow which is one of my best and hardest to do. People don't appreciate my work like you do. Well, it's time for me to get started – I hope you like it. Then I'll call it a day. See you tomorrow, my beach friend.

—24—

The One Hundred Yard Forecast

Recently, I have had four days without even a glimpse of the sun. The weather report was for four days of sun. What went wrong? How can the weather people be one hundred percent inaccurate?

Do they need bigger and better computers, more satellites or just more training? I think that they just don't understand how complex our weather along the shoreline can be.

The ocean temperatures can very from thirty-two degrees in the winter to eighty degrees during the summer. The wind can very from zero to 40 miles an hour. When these two forces meet, only God knows the result.

This is something that they will not admit but I see it every day. It is almost impossible to predict, but the weather people get on our air waves and give a forecast for the shore like it is written in stone.

I check their forecast each night to see what time I should arise, how I should dress and what kind of day I can expect to have on the beach.

Weather report for tomorrow: "Sunny all day." The next morning, I jumped out of bed and, yes, it is a sunny day. Off to the beach I go ready for a great day. Unfortunately, in two hours, the sun is gone. I rest my case. This happens far too often. I am an expert on this subject and my opinion cannot be debated.

In my fourteen years on the beach, the weather accuracy, which consists of wind speed, wind direction, clouds, sun and storms, it would not earn a grade higher than a "c." The forecasters must do better, so I am proposing a new system that shall be called, "The one hundred yard forecast." That is what the shore people want because that's really all we are interested in. What will the weather be like from the Boardwalk to the ocean? In this area it is a different world and all the beach people know this to be true. We want a separate forecast for this separate world and we want more than one sentence like "There will be an ocean breeze tomorrow." Beach people depend on the accuracy of the weather forecast. Only a detailed "one hundred yard forecast" will satisfy us!

—25—

Acceptance and Health

My journey on the beaches of Ocean City have taken me from depression to addiction and finally to acceptance. I now realize that for me happiness is about going to the beach every day. This is who I am. This is what I do.

The malls, casinos, libraries and gyms all have quality therapeutic value, but none of them take full advantage of Mother Nature's free, powerful and wondrous healing powers.

Doctors and researchers have for years debated the virtues of vitamin D, which comes in huge quantities, compliments of our precious sun. To me it is a no-brainer. I am 75 years young, and I have no aches or pains, nor do I take any pills or medicines. What more proof do they or I need? The sun an fresh air I breathe every day, plus eight months of body boarding from April to December, have certainly slowed down aging for me.

There will naturally be those doubters who would say that it is just good luck and good genes. But I wish they would all join me on this journey to the fountain of youth that I have found right here in Ocean City.

Coming off the beach with grandkids Emily, Nicholas and Kevin Dayton. If you get to the Boardwalk and it is still light out, you've left too early!

—26—

Beautiful Winter

It is a Friday night in the middle of January and I am in Harrah's Casino. I have been going there for over twenty years so the casino people know me well. "Nice tan," they yell as I walk by. "Just get back from Florida Earl?" "No, just sitting every day on the beach in Ocean City," I reply.

I make this point because I want people to know the great disparities in our winter weather. During the winter season, twenty-five percent of the days will be above normal temperatures, which means these days are warm enough for someone to maintain a tan during that time. This is especially true if there are three or four consecutive sunny days.

Many people put their beach chairs away too early and they will miss a lot of nice days. Come on down and try it. You will surely be in for a pleasant surprise.

—27—

Wicked Winter

It is 4 p.m. in the middle of January and I have just walked into my warm condo. I was on the beach for four hours of Hell battling 20-30 mile-an-hour winds, which swirled around my plastic tarp fortress.

The wind is blowing from the south off of the ocean, which means that 35° air is blowing at me on a day when the outdoor temperature didn't reach thirty. Believe me, it is very hard to describe this kind of a day that usually happens ten to twenty times each winter. Mother Nature is constantly thinking of ways to dislodge me from the beach.

It is her unlimited powers versus my headstrong resolve to see what weather condition can a beach bum handle. When she increases the wind or drops the temperature, I just put on more clothes. Today there are seven layers on the top three layers on the bottom, a hooded ski mask, heated socks and mittens. It is just about impossible to endure three hours on the beach unless you are covered from head to toe.

When I finally get set up on the beach behind my umbrella and tarps, I get out my newspaper, turn on the radio, pour my first cup of coffee, sit back on my beach chair and smile. I have once again beaten Mother Nature and she knows it. I am sure she will be thinking up a doozy for tomorrow!

—28—

Some Suggestions for God

I am sorry if it sounds like I am complaining. You know that I enjoy your fabulous beaches, which are really masterpieces. However, I have written a short list of improvements that you can easily perform with just a few small miracles when you are not busy with other things of course.

1. Do you think it would be possible to give us a bird that likes to eat flies? Lord! You can't imagine how annoying these little creatures can be. They can ruin one of your most beautiful days or even a whole week. Maybe if you made them taste more like chicken, it

would increase their chances of getting eaten. You could call the bird a "fly swallow" if you want. It is quite catchy.

2. Your summers are always beautiful, Lord! But last year we lost too many days because of rain and storms. Would it be at all possible to reschedule some of this weather to a later time, like between midnight and 6 a.m.? I know that you have to take care of the farmers first, but do whatever you can for your beach worshippers.

3. Lord! I am sure that you are aware of all the talk about global warming and since it is your globe, could you possibly hasten this warm weather because, quite frankly, I am running out of years. I am getting tired of sitting on the beach and trying to stay warm during these cold winters.

It is your universe and I heard that you move in mysterious ways, so I will be watching and waiting. Year-round seventy-degree ocean water would be nice too.

4. Lord! Have your noticed your beaches lately? Again, we had lost fifty percent of our beach sand in the first year of replenishment. We have got to break this crazy way of wasting money and spoiling the next two summers. We have got to break this cycle!

Would you consider working with our scientists and researchers to help them come up with better ways to save our beaches?

Like maybe, sand super glue, Velcro sand strips, Astro sand rugs or artificial sand?

—29—

Earl's Favorite Beach One-Liners, Retorts and Jokes

Beach umbrellas – weapons of mass destruction.

Beach Shovels – Very holy.

Never trust a flip flop.

Surfer marries jogger – waverunner.

Jetski – a Polish surfer.

What do they call a surfer in Iowa? "Lost."

What do they call a surfer who wants to be a bodyboard? "Smart."

What do sharks call surfers? "Food."

Did you ever see a happy jogger?

Swimming trunks can't swim.

Everyone should believe in something. One size fits all bikinis.

Why does a pizza always taste better on the beach? Because someone else is usually paying for it.

Why are flies so annoying on the beach? They learn from watching the seagulls.

When someone is drowning, why don't they yell S.O.S.?

All joggers should wear a number on their backs – 911.

Never be de-feeted by flip flops.

Did you hear about the jogger on the Boardwalk who got a ticket for "dogging it?"

Bodyboarders know how to lie down on the job.

What's the difference between a laughing gull and a rat? Nothing!

What do you get if you cross a laughing gull with a crab? A crab that giggles.

If bodyboarders had bigger feet they wouldn't need flippers.

Every once in a while, I get a "burst" to go back to work. Fortunately, it doesn't last too long.

Did you hear about the seagulls that went to the singles bar? They heard that a lot of "gulls" would be there.

Met a nice surfer out in the ocean today. One out of ten ain't bad.

I have a philosophy – only believe half of what you see on the beach. The other half is unbelievable.

I do not watch girls in bikinis on the beach. Yesterday there were three that I especially didn't look at.

There is more to life than just sitting on the beach. Yes! Laying on the beach.

I ran up to the Boardwalk when I heard that there was a half off bikini sale.

If you hang up your wet suit in a closet for two weeks, is it still called a wet suit?

We should have a newspaper for our beaches. Call it the "sandpaper."

A seagull walks into a pizza shop on the Boardwalk and says, "Give me a slice of pizza."
Pizza man: "That will be twenty dollars."
Seagull: "You must think I am very gull-ible."
Pizza man: "Do you want this pizza or not?"
Seagull: "Okay." Just put it on my bill."

Seagull walks into church to confess his "sins." The Priest gave him four our feathers.

Half of the people on the beach wish that the other half would leave.

The trouble with being retired and going to the beach is that as soon as you sit down on your beach chair, you are on the clock.

Jogging is only necessary if you have just robbed a bank.

How can an old geezer like me make out with a young

babe when these kids won't stop calling me Pop-Pop?

What do you get when you cross a crab with a clam? I don't know. But it sounds like a delicious soup.

There was an alcoholic on our beach looking for a sandbar.

It is alright to laugh at fat women wearing bikinis. Just don't point.

Surfer had a chance to go out with a good looking woman but the waves looked great so he went out with the tide.

A wave or a babe. It is not easy to be a surfer.

—30—

Lifeguard Humor

The best three jobs created by man for men.

1. Lifeguard

2. Lifeguard

3. Lifeguard

Any questions?

Lifeguards' favorite candy: Lifesavers.

How many lifeguards does it take to save a senior citizen? One! How many lifeguards does it take to save a babe? Eight!

Lifeboats must be renamed "playboats."

If someone doesn't want to be saved, does it still count as a save?

Did you ever see a lifeguard who wasn't smiling?

I saw a lifeguard save three people yesterday. I saw a born again Christian save ten people today.

Did you hear about the seagull that became a lifeguard? He never had one seagull drown while he was on duty.

Did you hear about the shark that wanted to be a lifeguard? He said that he would give an arm and leg to be one.

Lifeguard stand – A place where lifeguards SIT.

If lifeguards fail to make a rescue in their life boat, is it then called a death boat?

Favorite lifeguard cookie: Oar-E-Rows

—31—

The Beach Tag Game

Pretend you are sleeping.

Jump into the ocean.

Tell them you're a big eleven.

Go get pizza.

Tell them it only looks like you shave.

My dog ate the beach tags.

They're on mom's beach bag.

Atlantic City and Wildwood don't have beach tags.

Do you have a two hour tag?

Do you take Visa?

—32—

Talk of the Beach

Listen carefully and you're bound to hear some of the following comments floating on the salty breeze.

Why are those people feeding the seagull?

Is the tide going in or out? What's a tide?

*I think that I will go up and get a couple slices of pizza.
I'll start my diet when we get home.*

*I am on a diet. Just get me a slice of pizza, a large
French fries, a funnel cake and a diet soda.*

That seagull just took the sandwich right out of my hand!

I thought that you brought the sunblock.

I can't believe that we're going home tomorrow.

It's your turn to take Johnny to the bathroom.

I have a handkerchief bigger than that bikini.

I came sixty miles to boogie board and there are no waves.

The weather wasn't great this week but it was better than going to work.

How many times do I have to tell you kids – don't throw sand!

How many times do I have to tell you kids – Don't feed the seagulls!

Is someone smoking a cigar on the beach?

 Music to my ears?

I took my beach chair down and sat by the water. I could hear the music of the dancing waves that pounded on the sand. The sound of violins, a piano and drums rang through my ears...oops, sorry it was only someone's cell phone ringing!

—33—

You know it is going to be a bad day at the beach when:

The lifeguards blow their whistles at you while you're sitting in a beach chair.

You get caught in a rip current and you wave to the lifeguard and he waves back.

You purchase a beach tag and it expires at 2 p.m. that day.

A seagull dumps on your head and people tell you it means good luck.

You get hit with a football, a Frisbee and an umbrella and the people responsible give you a dirty look.

You go into the ocean with your boogie board and you forgot how to boogie.

The flies love the smell of your sunblock.

The guy sitting next to you is wearing a New York Giants football sweatshirt.

EAST *of the* BOARDWALK

It is windy and the beach umbrellas look like missiles
flying over Baghdad.

The beach tag people are dressed in S.W.A.T. team
uniforms.

The gnats set up headquarters on your head.

You take your wife to the beach and she takes your
credit card to the boardwalk.

The guy next to you says that he is on a tsunami
watch.

You return from a swim and find three strangers sitting
under your umbrella.

—34—

The Game

The people who take the time to find me on the beach at Plymouth Place do it because they think that I am a famous person. My friends who sit with me also think that I am famous. If this is true, I must tell you that a lot of hard work has been put into my "fame."

When you see me sitting on the beach doing nothing that is really only a small part of my beach life. Most of my day is spent trying to stay in excellent shape. If I weren't in excellent shape then I couldn't be the person that I am. It is that simple.

My biggest fear is developing a problem with my back or limbs, which would certainly finish my beach bum career. To push and pull a cart that weighs forty pounds in the winter and seventy pounds in the summer requires a lot of strength. If I did get hurt, then my only option would be suicide!

On the beach I have found the secret and format for staying healthy. I call it "The Game." I call it that because to me what I do coming and going from the beach and also setting up all my "stuff" is a game. In my life I've never liked to lose at anything I did and is there a better game to win than the game of life?

"The Game" always starts at the beginning of January on the goal line and finishes on the other goal line in late December. The object is for me to get a minimum of 350 days on the beach. If I am successful, then it is a win for me. Last year (2011), I made it to the beach 356 days – a win!

What does it mean to win? Well it means that I had to walk 200,000 yards just to get from my condo to the beach and back, pulling my cart. There are seven steps from the beach to the boardwalk, which means that I had to pull my cart up and down 5,000 steps. I raised and planted 600 eight-foot umbrellas. I could go on and on but I think that you would agree, those numbers are impressive for any age and I was seventy-five. It certainly proves that I am famous for doing the impossible.

The Game works for me. It has made me healthy and strong but probably won't work for you. You must find your own game, one that is fun to do, and can clearly show you results.

Don't consider running – you will just wear out your body parts. The people who encourage you to run are all orthopedic doctors.

Never look back or take a step backwards. Status quo is okay but never retreat. Once you do "The Game" will be over and it will be a loss.

—35—

Number One Beach Bum?

When I first retired to Ocean City in 1995, it didn't take me long to realize that I had much to learn about living at the shore. There were many assumptions about how things were and many misconceptions about how they actually are. There was one assumption that changed my life.

I had been sitting on the beach for many years and I "assumed" that since Ocean City had a lot of retirees, then there must be someone like me sitting on every beach. I never traveled north or south from my spot at Plymouth Place and I could not very well go to City Hall and get a list of beach bums.

Newspaper articles and my book made my beach bum story grow. One day a friend of mine asked me to do an interview for a website that he was putting together. I agreed to this and he started asking me questions. "Are you Ocean City's number one beach bum?" he asked. Well, he caught me off guard with the question. But I knew that unless I would make such a claim, then Ocean City would never know if I was or not.

"Yes!" I said and then he got me again. "In the history of Ocean City?" he asked. This one might have been a reach but there was no going back now, so once again I said, "yes!" I had wanted to have someone ask me those questions for years and finally I was going to find the answers. If there were anyone out there who thought that I was over-stepping my area of expertise about beach bums in Ocean City, then I would surely hear from them.

I repeated this claim to the Atlantic City Press and they ran with it in an article about me. My phone did not ring and I received no threatening letters from any lawyers. The "Press" was still not convinced of my beach bum claim so they asked all year round beach bums to contact the paper. Some people did contact them, but the Press told me that they were not in the same league or on the same level as my story. They said that I would not be mentioned in their article on year-round beach bums but instead they would feature me separately in another piece on another day. They did and my story continued to grow while the doubters started to shrink.

I have no doubts about being number one beach bum in Ocean and yes, also in the history of Ocean City.

—36—

Number One Beach Bum in the World!

(In all four seasons)

Now that I was number one beach bum in New Jersey, I decided to expand my claim even further. After much thought it seemed logical to assume that being a year-round beach bum was not a really popular profession, especially during the winter months.

The question is "why would anyone want to do such a thing?" I have been doing it for 17 years. Just try it for 14 days when the temperature is below thirty and the wind is blowing. It is simply too hard to do.

You need to have many good reasons to do all four seasons – one or two will not pull you through the winter. I did have many things going for me. I had worked outside as a construction worker so sitting on the beach was a piece of cake. I was retired and didn't have to work and it only took three minutes to get to the beach from my beach block condo. The death of my wife was, of course, the driving motive that reinforced my decision to spend each day on the beach. I liked what I was doing. It was fun and interesting. I've always told people that I was the perfect storm – meaning many things had to line up in a row for me to accomplish this crazy lifestyle.

To think that there is someone else in the world doing all four seasons on the beach is almost unthinkable. So I have proclaimed myself number one in the world until proven otherwise. This theory worked in New Jersey and I am sure it will work nationally.

—37—

Recognition

The Acknowledgment of Achievement

Are you looking for a good place to hide? Well, I think that I have found the perfect place and it is right in the center of Ocean City. Why am I so sure that it is a good place to hide? Because I sat there at Plymouth Place for fourteen years and no one knew that I was there – except my friends, of course.

Fourteen years, five thousand days and thirty-five thousand hours and I was Mr. Cellophane. I sat there almost every day, setting records that will never be equaled or broken by any four-season beach bum. If Osama Bin Laden had known about this spot, he might still be alive.

But things were about to change because I was going to write a book about my many years on the beach in Ocean City.

In June of 2010, my book was first published and I was ready to sell a book about the beach that would excite the minds of all beachgoers. With the help of three newspaper articles – two from the *Atlantic City Press* and one from the *Philadelphia Inquirer*, my story took wing and flew out of Ocean City into all of South Jersey and most of Pennsylvania.

After 14 years of silence, my long overdo hope of being recognized was now starting to happen. This interesting story of a man's passion for sun and sand exposed me as the expert on all beach activities from sand to surf.

That was many months ago, but I am still reaping the benefits of those same newspaper articles. During a summer day it is not unusual to have three or four people seek me out at my spot on Plymouth Place. They come to shake my hand, take pictures and wait for me to spin stories about the beach.

They bestow accolades on me that surely were not meant for a retired pipefitter who wrote one book.

I will always be thankful to the newspapers that ran my story, for they have the power to decide the success or failure of a book. Fortunately they thought that I had a good and interesting story to tell. They gave me recognition.

—38—

Expanded Recognition

It was a cold, snowy and windy day in December of 2010. The snow was not just coming down, it was blowing sideways up Plymouth Place, towards the ocean. In my many years as a beach bum, I had learned never to judge the harshness of any storm from my condo window. My plan was to always get dressed and see if it was possible, not just to get on to the beach, but to stay there for the required three hours.

Eight out of ten times, I would see that it was possible to beat Mother Nature's fury. That day was no exception, so I proceeded to start putting on my layers of clothing.

It was 11 a.m. when the phone rang. "Hello," I said. "Is this Earl Paul of Ocean City?" someone asked. "Yes," I answered. "This is KYW Radio in Philadelphia and we were just sitting around having a coffee break when we said "I wonder if that guy in Ocean City is going to go to the beach today?" I explained to him my plan for going to the beach on bad days and that I was almost ready to try it.

This was certainly the pinnacle of my recognition. A radio station seventy miles away in another city wanted to know if I was going to the beach. They knew about my life from following the stories on Google and You Tube.

After fourteen years I was recognized and I hung up knowing that now my beach bum story wasn't just a shore thing.

—39—

Touching Recognition

It was late September 2011 about five o'clock in the afternoon and I was sitting alone on the beach. I saw an elderly lady having trouble walking towards me in the soft sand. When she got to where I was sitting, she said, "Are you the one who wrote the book?" "Yes," I answered, hoping she meant "East of the Boardwalk." "Do you want to purchase one?" I asked.

"Yes," she said. So I told her to wait there and I would return from my condo with a book in five minutes, which I did.

"Do you live in Ocean City?" I asked her as I signed the book. "No!" she said. "I am 83-years-old and I just drove two hours from Burlington County to get here. I saw the newspaper article about you and I knew that I had to come here today. My husband died three years ago and today is the anniversary of his death. I knew that I had to come here and get your book."

I handed her the book and she turned to walk away. I yelled to her, "Hey! What's your name?" But she did not turn around. I can only hope that she might find something in my book that made her trip worthwhile.

I went back to my beach chair and sat down. I knew that this was a special moment for my book and me.

—40—

Unexpected Recognition

In December of 2011, I received a phone call from someone who said she represented "The Friends of the Ocean City Library." She asked me if I would be interested in being the guest speaker at their 3rd annual "Authors Tea" to be held at the Flanders Hotel in Ocean City on May 5th. There would be 140 people in attendance.

This was the opportunity that I thought would never come – a chance to tell my beach bum story to the people of Ocean City. I immediately accepted her invitation.

I couldn't believe that they had selected a 75-year-old retired beach bum for such a wonderful honor. How did they know that an old guy like me would remember to be there? I have trouble remembering where my car keys are.

However, I am an Ocean City guy sitting on an Ocean City beach and I had written a book about the Ocean City beaches. We would be perfect together!

They requested that I do thirty minutes and I welcomed this unbelievable moment to promote the beach bum and his book. This was another one of those miracles that just seemed to happen and it certainly was a gift from God. This was going to raise my recognition level tremendously in Ocean City. Thanks to the wonderful people who thought me worthy of this honor, and thanks to the people and friends of the Ocean City Library for having me at your affair.

—41—

Divine Intervention

It was an unusually warm Sunday in January 2012. I chose to sit on the beach rather than watch a football play-off game on TV. It was too nice to be indoors so I sat there sunning myself and writing for the next edition of my book.

While I was writing, it came to me that another chapter, along with a few pictures would be needed before I could consider my work completed. I tried to think of something but nothing came to my mind, so I put it off for another day. Little did I know that it would happen in less than twenty-four hours.

It was a gray and drizzly Monday morning, about 11:30 a.m. I was standing with my back to the ocean, talking to a friend who was just passing by. She looked over my shoulder and said, "What is that out in the water?" This was usually my specialty since I was an expert on such questions. I turned around and saw a large brownish object that looked like a floating house. It was about a half mile from the beach and seemed to be drifting in our direction.

I grabbed my binoculars off of my cart and proceeded to walk to the rock jetty that would take me one hundred yards closer to this strange object. It was now within one hundred yards and with my binoculars it became more obvious that it was a whale.

It had been hard to identify it as a whale because its stomach, which was the size of a four-foot beach ball, had come out of its body. When I looked through the glasses, I saw a head and a giant beach ball beside its head. Quite a sight!

Now the whale was right at the jetty and it was going to be on "my" beach in minutes. I ran as quickly as I could to get my camera back at the condo so I could take pictures of this prehistoric creature that had come to us for this once in a lifetime occurrence. The odor at my condo, which is approximately one hundred yards from the whale, would take your breath and your appetite away. It was beyond words.

When I ran back to the jetty, I saw that a crowd of about fifty people had already gathered and before this was all over, five to ten thousand people would visit the sight. It was something to see a sixty-foot whale, which was obviously dead, being tossed around in the shallow waters twenty feet from the sand. It was low tide, so the water was going out, but soon the tide would be turning, bringing stronger surf and bigger waves.

This started to happen shortly before dark and the ocean became rougher with waves up to six feet pounding the poor giant, making him look like he was alive and trying to swim away.

The ocean and the waves began to lift and pound this twenty-ton mammal bringing it further and further up onto the beach. Darkness came but it did not slow the number of people who were scurrying down from the boardwalk to see the whale, that had now made the radio and television news. This was an event everyone wanted to say they witnessed – the whale on the beach in Ocean City.

At 10 p.m. there were still around one hundred people on the beach with flashlights and floodlights shining on the carcass as the waves tossed it around like a big toy!!

In the morning I saw that the high tide had lifted the whale way up the beach. The tide then receded leaving the full length of the whale exposed for everyone to photograph and admire its great size. I only wish the hundreds of people who came that day would have had the same opportunity as I did to put a mental picture in your head of this scene while it was still fresh in my mind.

At 11 o'clock they closed the beach to all spectators, which I thought was a mistake because it was a once in a lifetime sight that many people never got a chance to witness! The people were restricted to the boardwalk where the high sand dunes hid the whale from their sight.

The Marine Mammal Stranding Center came on the scene to determine the cause of death and to help with the dismantling of the whale. They estimated that it was dead for about one week, which coincided with a report of a dead whale that floated by Long Island, New York. A boat's propeller probably struck it. And I would agree because when I first saw the whale, its face was badly cut.

They identified the whale as a fin whale, 60 feet in length and probably fully-grown. It is the second largest whale. Only the blue whale is bigger.

Now the gross and sad part was about to begin with the cutting apart of the whale's body with large three-foot long blades. They cut it up into large pieces that continually slipped out of the grasp of the large front-end loaders as they tried to lift them onto a dump truck.

The pieces were loaded and taken down to the north end of the city and buried near the bridge. They couldn't finish it that day, so the last eight feet of the whale was still there the next morning. It took two hours to cut up and remove the final piece of what was once a magnificent mammal. The workers tried their best to clean and cover up the bloody mess, which had leaked onto the sand. But five weeks after, there was still a smell of death coming from the area where the whale had lain.

By mid-morning, they were all gone. The people, two front-end loaders and the large dump truck had finally left "my" beach and once again things were back to wintertime normalcy.

It was almost like a dream. This creature of the sea had drifted down the coast of New Jersey and then made a right hand turn at the 7th Street jetty, which landed the whale thirty yards from where I sit every day.

My friends and I will never question the logic of this happening. We just call it divine intervention. No wind or storm would have changed the course of this whale. It was just meant to arrive at Plymouth Place.

So now I had more material for my book, pictures of the whale, and I am probably the only one with two bone parts as souvenirs. It was a crazy and exciting forty-eight hours and it just added to a long list of miracles since I arrived in Ocean City.

—42—

The Whale: Why My Beach?

He thought that he could pick up a date at one of our many "sandbars."

He was looking for his blubber and sister.

He didn't know that Ocean City was a dry town.

He thought that the water park was still open.

His GPS was not working.

He had a whale of a tale to tell.

It was winter and his "tail was told."

He never met a beach bum in the winter.

Divine intervention told him to make a right hand turn at the 7th Street jetty.

A footnote:

Something very strange happens every day since they cut up the whale. Almost every dog that walks by the area where the whale was sliced into pieces, stops and starts to roll on their backs. It seems to cause a reaction from them like catnip for a cat. The owners stop and stare at their dogs wondering what they are doing. At first I thought that it was just one or two dogs, but almost every dog that walks by that spot does seem to get high on the smell. Doesn't do much for me!

—43—
Commandments of the Beach

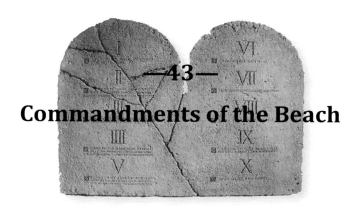

Thou shall listen to the man with the whistle for he will lead you from the dangerous waters.

Let the beach people stop and worship at the trash cans before they leave the beach.

There shall be no ill words spoken against the beach tag people for they know not what they do.

Thou shall not try to kill the seagull that just stole your sandwich.

Thou shall not covet they neighbor's sand.

Pray on the beach. But don't expect that girl on the next blanket to give you a second look.

Beautiful creatures in swimwear: choose modesty as your virtue.

Worship and wear only Phillies and Eagles logos on your tee shirts.

There shall be no laughing or snickering at the people with weird tattoos in mysterious places.

Forgive the rudeness and ignorance of a few on the beach for they shall be leaving on Saturday morning.

Lead the children to the waters and addict them to the fantasy world of sun, sand and ocean.

Let the beach people run down to the water. Only next time use the bathrooms at the Music Pier.

—44—

Looking Back

Bow Wow City Chapters

I always thought that the pen was mightier than the sword, but my book had absolutely no influence in preventing people from running their dogs on the beach. In fact it has even gotten worse. It used to be 50% of the dogs were off of the leash, now it is 75%. Some days I do not see any dogs on a leash. No ticket! No fear!

In my chapters on dogs, I told you that 100% of the people who run their dogs do not clean up the mess that pollutes our beaches. What more do the city officials want to know?

Beach Etiquette Chapter

Many people have asked me to take my beach etiquette ideas to the city. My ideas are helpful and well considered but unless someone knows what it is like to

East of the Boardwalk

sit on a crowded beach, they will never understand why it is so important.

Global Warming – Page 148

I asked God to please speed up global warming because, quite frankly, I am running out of decades. My prayers were answered in 2011-2012 with one of the warmest falls and winters on record. There were many days that felt like summer temperatures of fifty and sixty became the norm.

Also, after two years of stopping in December, year round body boarding returned to my beach bum life. Last year the ocean reached a low of 32 degrees. This year it never went below 41 degrees. I just hope that the almighty one does not skip over my beach replenishment request, also on page 148.

Get ready for a lot of sand

Kevin Dayton

My pop pop

If you don't think this is amazing then you're crazy! Have you ever heard of a pop pop that goes to the beach 365 days a year? Didn't think so. During the summer he comes all the way to Somedale to pick us up for fun in the sun in Ocean City. My siblings and I always look foward to the weekends.

My pop pop is also writting a book about his life. I admire him for writting this book because, He is taking time out of his summer to write this book. The book is about his life. If you sat down and talked to him about his life you would be amazed. He says it's the perfect life, and everyone agrees with him.

My pop pop is now 73 and in better shape than a 60 year old. He's been body boarding since he was 60, and still doing it now. He was the one who got me and my siblings into bodyboarding. He is a very smart and understandable guy. This is why I picked my pop pop to be the person I admire.

2007 letter to me from my grandson Kevin as a
"Who do I admire?" school assignment.

—45—

Big Blue Christmas Eve

Hello, Earl. It's Christmas Eve and I didn't know if you would be out to play with me today. This is a busy time of the year for me and I haven't had a lot of time to make up some nice sets of waves for you to ride. I know that you will like the ones I have made for you. I am getting a little colder. Have you noticed?

I hope it won't stop you from bodyboarding. I miss you when you don't come down to have some fun. I see that you have a new wet suit on. Is that a Christmas present? Well, I'd better stop talking. You're missing a lot of good waves. Okay Buddy, Go get this one – it's a beauty!

See you later bodyboarder.

—46—

"Off Season" – Winter

I know that you will find it hard to feel sorry for me; after all, I only have to get to the beach everyday. A short time ago the beach was alive with many moms and dads watching their kids playing in the sand. Now everyone has left and I will be alone for a long time.

It is now just a pigeon and two seagulls who will entertain and annoy me. I am a special beach bum, but I am also only human. I must adjust my mind to these changes or the loneliness can cause anyone to be depressed. Then I realize that this is actually a blessing because it separates me from all the other beach bums in the world.

Also it gives me a chance to see many of my summer beach friends who will drive to Ocean City just to see if I am sitting at my spot on Plymouth Place. They know that I will be there and it is important for me not to disappoint them, which I seldom do! They know that I am the real thing so I don't want or need any validation by the Guinness Book of World Records. I cannot prove that I am and they cannot prove that I'm not. My friends believe that I am number one so that's good enough for me.

It will usually take two or three weeks before my mind starts to adjust to the new winter season. I accept that it will be lonely, cold, windy and sometimes snowy but it is doable.

I do have the physical and mental strength to get through those difficult months from December to March. At times it will seem almost beyond the limits of what my body can endure. That is when I must make the decision to surrender to old man winter for health and safety reasons, but I can miss only 15 days. After a week of sitting out in twenty degree temperatures I once again realize that no one will ever even try to beat my record of days on the beach in all four seasons.

—47—

Late Fall – The Beginning of the Lonely Time

It is the last week in November and the long winter months are about to show their ugly face. Yes! The winters are very long and sometimes very cold on the beach. Winter will usually last five or six months, not the three months that you see on your calendar. This is because of the cold ocean water temperatures of this large body of water. Because it is so large, it will take a long time to heat up and a long time to cool down, which is why we can still be cold in the month of May.

I have been through sixteen of these winters so this is just another one of the four seasons in the life of the world's number one beach bum. This is the crazy life that I have chosen and the life that keeps my mind and body healthy, strong and mobile. Now I cannot stop or even think about stopping because of the view that I see every morning when I get to the beach. It is like starting a new life every day and just like a snowflake, no two mornings are alike. The ocean, sand and sky change and wonderful pictures are planted in my mind that will last forever, even after my beach days are over. This makes me feel like the luckiest man in Ocean City. I just wish that more of the retired people would realize that the Fountain of Youth can be found on the beaches. Learn how to enjoy each day and no place is more enjoyable than the beach.

—48—
If my umbrella could talk!

"When are you going to wash me? The seagulls are doing their best to make me look crappy. You haven't washed me in five weeks. I have some pride you know."

"Do your friends have to smoke? My colors will fade from the second-hand smoke."

"Yo girls! Come on over and sit in my shade. You're getting kind of red. Works every time!"

"Put me down, it's raining. I'm a shade umbrella."

"You're sitting in the shade and my butt is 120 degrees

Don't they know that is illegal in Ocean City! Shame! I always thought that this was a dry town."

"Do I have to go into the bag when we leave? I have nightmares about it."

"I heard that they are renting out my brothers and sisters on our beach. How low can they get?"

"Look out! Three umbrellas are learning to fly!"

"When are we going home? I have been up since early this morning."

"Ouch! That is the third time that I have been hit with a Frisbee. Aren't you going to chase them you wimp?"

"Soon the season will be over and I will take my place in the basement next to my friend, the hot water heater."

"How did I get stuck with a beach bum who will use me every day? My friends last 10 years. I'll be lucky to make it 10 months!"

"Will you please stop telling people that my nationality is pole-ish!"

—49—

Questions I am asked that I don't know the answers to.

Why do we have thousands of shells on our beach that are cutting vacationers' feet? This is the fifth year in a row. How about next time giving us some sand?

Why are the dunes thirty yards and the beaches twenty yards?

Why aren't there any fish in the ocean anymore?

Where did the mountains of seaweed go?

Where are all of the jellyfish?

Where do we sit in the third year of a beach replenishment?

Why do they plant grass on the dunes? Will it last five minutes or ten minutes when Sandy returns?

Why don't seagulls eat food from the sea?

—50—

Why are you sitting so close to me?

The number one problem on our beach and everybody else's beach will never be solved in 2014 or even 3014. There are no fines or penalties for putting your beach "stuff" right next to another person's stuff: The correct distance should be a minimum of three feet of space. When someone gets closer than that, the urge to kill can grow real.

Why do they put themselves so close is—and always will be—a mystery to me, who has seen hundreds of beach goers even touching another person's belongings. If we could gather the names and phone numbers of this mass of impolite people, maybe we could find out what makes them so unaware of their annoying actions. It doesn't even matter if the beach is empty; they still feel the need to smother you.

—51—

I just don't get it: The Surrey

It was a sunny summer Saturday morning and the grandkids and I were excited because we were going to take our first ride on the famous surrey.

If you are from Iowa, the surrey is a small army surplus tank that can hold up to six people, which means this monster can weigh a half-ton. It is feared by all people out walking on the Boardwalk. When they see one traveling at an unsafe speed as it makes its way through the crowds, people dive for cover.

We rented our first surrey and thought that the fun would start as we whizzed up the Boardwalk. I was already having second thoughts about this activity because I felt like no one else was pedaling. We certainly were not whizzing up the Boardwalk on this day that was supposed to be fun. It took us ten minutes to go one hundred yards, ten feet at a time. Pedal – brake – stop – pedal – brake – stop – etc. You get the picture.

When we got to the Music Pier, a summer policeman pulled us over and said that we would have to leave the Boardwalk because we had too many violations with our surrey.

1 – Hit two people!
But I found out later that the x-rays were negative.

2 – Totaled three bikes!
They were in our lane.

3 – Dented four city trash cans!
They were trash anyway.

4 – Scared the Hell out of one hundred people.
Made points with the Holy One.

I realized that the fun started when we returned the surrey. The kids never asked to do it again. You won't do this more than once without watching NASCAR for driving tips.

—52—
Dear Sun...

*B*rightest star in the daytime sky, shine on me like the medicine ball that I know you are. We have spent thousands of hours together on the beach and my love for you always makes my heart beat faster as your brilliant warm rays shine down on me.

I know that you must travel around the world as your job requires you to do, and yes I am jealous. Do you think of me when I don't see you for three or four days? Are you flirting with other beach bums?

Sorry if I question your love for me but I just miss you when you're away.

It may sound selfish but I only wish that I could slow your trip across the daytime sky. Thanks for keeping me warm during the cold months and happy during the hot summer. You will always be the center of my universe because I know that it is impossible to live without you. Only you, God and I know about our love affair, which makes me rush to the beach each morning. Some day I will tell everyone about it, but now it is just our secret.

—53—

Handicap Access – Where?

I believe that the people who run the city do not spend much time on our beaches. If they did they would see how people struggle getting up and down our steps with baby coaches, wagons and wheelchairs. And how about our senior citizens? If they witness what I see every day, they would run home, get some wood, a hammer and some nails and start building ramps at every entrance.

If you think that I am wrong, you don't want to admit that this makes sense. The city could have corrected this 1970, 1980 and 1990. Now they say it will cost too much. I don't want to hear about the handicap laws. I just want someone to stand up and correct this sad situation.

—54—

I just don't get it: Bicycles

The surrey turned out not to be the exciting adventure that we hoped it would be. I said to the kids, "Let's try riding our bikes." Right away I knew that this would be better because we all had a bike so this would not cost me any money.

It was a nice Sunday morning as we gathered on the Boardwalk ready to "whiz" down the boards. It was so crowded with vacationers that whizzing was not going to be possible. The surrey was able to travel ten feet but the bikes were about to go twelve feet. A two-foot difference. Wow! Why didn't we try this first?

Pedal – brake – stop, pedal – brake – stop! Anyone for dodge ball? I asked the kids to try to stick together but even super glue couldn't keep us all together.

The city spends a lot of time and money painting lanes on the Boardwalk which no one uses. Save the money and just paint "women and children first."

The kids never ask to do this again either which should tell you how much fun they had. I'll wait until October.

—55—

Happiness is...

Seagull, sun, umbrella

Living year round in Ocean City.

Not owning a metal detector.

When the lifeguards return in June.

Celebrating all holidays by the sea.

Spending your golden years living at the ocean's edge.

A beach chair and an umbrella and throw in some
sand.

Meeting new friends each summer on the beach.

Missing the Doo-Dah Parade.

Sitting on the beach and watching the fireworks on the
4th of July.

The New Year's Day Polar Bear Plunge.

The view of the ocean that I will never take for
granted.

Having a nine AM coffee on the beach in the summer.

Taking a 2 PM snooze on the beach.

April 30th – when dogs can no longer be on our beaches.

Watching the morning raising of the flag and the playing of the national anthem in front of the water park every morning at 9:20 AM. God bless Jimmy.

Missing the "Night in Venice."

Spending twelve hours a day on the beach.

—56—

War on the beach at Plymouth Place

I have just sent a letter to seagull headquarters stating that all seagulls must withdraw from my beach at Plymouth Place. There will be no talks or communication between the enemy and me since I will not negotiate with these known terrorists.

If they fail to vacate my beach by January the 1st, 2016, then sanctions will be put into place and their supply of pizza will be greatly reduced, followed by other cuts in their food supply.

This is war! We will fight them on the beach and at the trash cans until they stop occupying my territory. I have tried to make peace with them, but they just keep laughing at me!

—57—

Just have to get some things off my chest.

Why do birds suddenly appear every time you are near? You probably just bought a cup of French fries on the Boardwalk.

There are lots of surfing lessons given on our beaches. Why doesn't someone give lessons on how to get a kite up in the air?

I am a very popular person on the beach. Every morning when I come down I get a lot of waves.

You can be fined 5 hundred dollars if you get caught feeding a seagull. But the seagulls can steal food out of your hand and there is nothing that you can do. It is called the seagulls' "Bill of Rights."

At the next beach replenishment can we please have just sand instead of broken pieces of shells?

The number one safety problem on our beaches is still the notorious and dangerous fifteen dollar umbrella. The people do not want to spend there money on a well made umbrella so they put every at risk on our beaches. This will continue until someone has a serious head injury. If they would put motors on those lifeboats we would need fewer lifeguards.

Seagulls take stalking lessons.

Lifeguards never want to drown their troubles.

Some day there will be no beach tags on the Ocean City beaches. And someday elephants will fly!

I need someone to pull strings for me on the beach.

Many summer vacationers come to the beach and make a blanket statement about their territory!

I live in my own little world. But that's okay because God put me here.

After years on the beach I have proven that the black-headed bird that annoys us all summer – the laughing gull – is the dumbest animal on the planet. I have given them many tests to prove my point and they never even make it to zero. They cannot think or reason. Those French fries are melting their brains!

Spring is only the 10th of June on the beach! The 11th is actually summer. Spring is just one day!

I have tried for three years to honor our lifeguards on August 1st. After much talk, the city has agreed to celebrate this event every June 31st. I'll believe it when it happens. It sounds kind of fishy to me!

They will soon have to stop putting the stand up signs on the Boardwalk, "No dogs allowed on Boardwalk." The dogs and their owners are tripping and falling over the signs. Very bad for public relations.

Let's do away with the fifty signs on the Boardwalk – "No dogs allowed" – and replace it with just one large sign. "No Dogs Allowed."

No Warnings; No Excuses; $100 fine; End of problem.

—58—

The Second Time Around

What could be better than to live a full and happy life? The answer is two full and happy lives! The problem is that only a small number of us will ever get that chance to live another life.

The first requirement is to live long enough. Then something must happen to start you on another journey into your second life.

I was fortunate to have the opportunity to choose the beach for my second life and I never looked back. I spent sixty happy years working and raising four kids and it was full of fun and good times.

Now my plate is clear and I am coming up on twenty years of my second life. I believe that God has rewarded me with this gift of sun and sand because I have always made an effort to be a good person and he wanted me to spend the rest of my days on his pile of sand at Plymouth Place.

I would never try to compare the two lives, because one life lasted six decades and the other is still a work in progress.

If you life a long life and you don't have the desire to start over, that's okay, but read my book and come visit me in Ocean City. You might want to reach out for that golden ring. Sometimes it happens twice.

—59—

The End

Everything in our life has a beginning and an end – including this book. I am ready to bring "East of the Boardwalk" to its end by not adding any more chapters to the book. It is time to put the book to bed before my words about the beach and my life in Ocean City become repetitious.

This book really is a success since it has sold over seven hundred copies. I will continue to devote my time and energy towards promoting what I have already written. I have no doubt that it will shortly reach the one thousand copy mark because there is no other book like "East of the Boardwalk!"

Until we're together again...